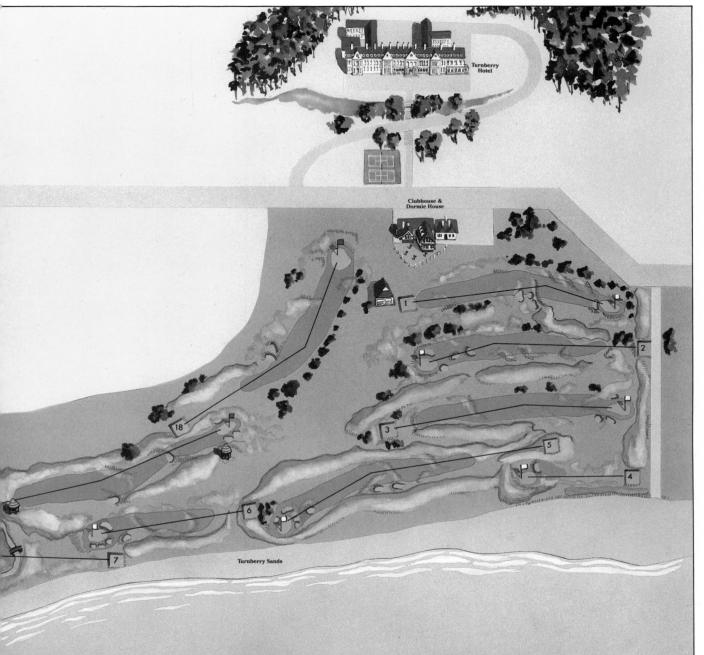

Turnberry Hotel

Clubhouse & Dormie House

Turnberry Sands

Turnberry Bay

CARD OF THE CHAMPIONSHIP COURSE

Hole	Name	Yards	Par	Hole	Name	Yards	Par
1	Ailsa Craig	350	4	10	Dinna Fouter	452	4
2	Mak Siccar	428	4	11	Maidens	177	3
3	Blaw Wearie	462	4	12	Monument	448	4
4	Woe-be-Tide	167	3	13	Tickly Tap	411	4
5	Fin'me oot	441	4	14			4
6	Tappie Toorie	222	3	15			
7	Roon the Ben	528	5	16			
8	Goat Fell	427	4	17			
9	Bruce's Castle	455	4	18			
	Out	3480	35				

THE OPEN
CHAMPIONSHIP
1986

SPRINGWOOD BOOKS
ASCOT, BERKSHIRE

THE OPEN
CHAMPIONSHIP
1986

WRITERS

RENTON LAIDLAW
NORMAN MAIR
ALISTER NICOL
DONALD STEEL
MICHAEL WILLIAMS
MARK WILSON

PHOTOGRAPHERS

LAWRENCE LEVY
BRIAN MORGAN

EDITOR

BEV NORWOOD

AUTHORISED BY THE
CHAMPIONSHIP COMMITTEE
OF THE ROYAL AND ANCIENT
GOLF CLUB OF ST. ANDREWS

©1986 The Championship Committee Merchandising Limited

First published 1986
Springwood Books Ltd., Ascot, Berkshire

All rights reserved

Typesetting by Skelly Typography, Inc.
Cleveland, Ohio

Printed in Great Britain by Jolly & Barber Ltd, Rugby

Statistics of 115th Open Championship
produced on a Burroughs Computer System

All photographs taken on FUJI professional films

Page 8 courtesy of Jack Nicklaus,
from *The Greatest Game of All* (Simon & Schuster, 1969)

Photographs of Turnberry by Ronny Jaques/Gourmet
©1986 The Conde Nast Publications Inc.

Turnberry Ailsa course map
by Frank Bissette

Springwood Books
Ascot, Berkshire

ISBN 0-86254-129-8

CONTENTS

THE CHAMPIONSHIP COMMITTEE

A. J. LOW, *Chairman*

G. M. SIMMERS, O.B.E., *Deputy Chairman*

J. R. BOARDMAN

Sir ROBIN CATER

J. P. GRANT

T. E. D. HARKER

R. D. JAMES

Dr. D. W. NISBET

M. J. REECE

W. G. N. ROACH

R. T. ROBINSON

Sir ROSS STAINTON, C.B.E.

T. B. TAYLOR

H. THOMSON

Additional Member

E. A. C. DENHAM

Council of National Golf Unions

M. F. BONALLACK, O.B.E., *Secretary*

W. G. WILSON, *Deputy Secretary*

D. HILL, *Championship Secretary*

INTRODUCTION

By A. J. Low

Chairman of Championship Committee
Royal and Ancient Golf Club of St. Andrews

Though the weather was less than ideal, the 115th Open Championship at Turnberry was a memorable occasion which the Championship Committee of the Royal and Ancient Golf Club is pleased to have recorded in this third annual publication.

In the winds of the first day the average score soared above 78 strokes. Then Greg Norman, our eventual champion, returned a 63 on the second day to equal the lowest score in Open Championship history. He held a one-stroke advantage after the rainy third round and came home five strokes clear on the marvellous fourth day when, at last, the beautiful setting of Turnberry was seen at its best.

We congratulate Greg Norman on his performance, and we also offer our sincere thanks to the contributors to this publication which commemorates his wonderful victory.

Alistair Low

A. J. Low

When the time came for me to get to my feet and receive the trophy, I got so choked up that tears came into my eyes and I couldn't talk. This had never happened to me before at a presentation. As I stood there, I began to understand why I was so overcome with emotion. Very simply, I hadn't been at all sure that I would ever be up there standing beside that trophy – a high-ball player like me who couldn't handle hard linksland fairways and who had always found a way to lose in the British Open and probably would continue to. "Excuse me," I said to the people gathered for the presentation. "Do you mind if I just enjoy this moment?" When I resumed speaking, it all came easily.

Jack Nicklaus, 1966

FOREWORD

By Greg Norman

I've never cried on a golf course before, but walking down the seventeenth and eighteenth in the final round at Turnberry, I was fighting to hold back the tears. Especially on the seventeenth. When I hit my approach in there about five or six feet, the people went crazy. That's the dominant reflection I have from winning the 115th Open Championship at Turnberry. The People. They fell in behind us during the last one hundred and fifty yards of the seventeenth and the walk to that green was just as strong an emotion as during the traditional rugby scrum on the eighteenth fairway because by that time I realised and convinced myself that the championship was mine as long as I signed the scorecard correctly.

Truth be known, even when I was sitting at the presentation table waiting for them to give me the trophy, I was so scared I had done something wrong with the card. I just knew somebody was going to walk up and say, "Gee, I'm sorry, Greg, but we can't give this to you after all." I was petrified that I might have signed the card wrong or put down my nine-hole score in the box for the ninth hole.

It had all been so long in coming and after all the frustrations of the near-misses in the U.S. Open and U.S. Masters, I couldn't believe I was sitting there in the champion's chair and they were going to give me the championship trophy. It was only when I had that wonderful old loving cup in my hands that I convinced myself I had truly and irrevocably won.

Walking down the eighteenth was, in a word, overwhelming.

To get a standing ovation in any walk of life – professor, lawyer, president, whatever – is a wonderful experience. Winning a golf championship is a wonderful thing, especially when it's the British Open, which is the true Open, the oldest championship in golf and in the country where I first won a professional tournament in Europe after venturing away from my native Australia. But the true reward is the emotions of the moment – the emotions of the spectators, of my friends, of the other players like Jack Nicklaus and Bruce Devlin and Fuzzy Zoeller and all the other people who got wrapped up in it just as much as I did. The emotion, to me, was the greatest thrill of winning the Open because I've never before experienced it to that degree.

Greg Norman

115th
OPEN CHAMPIONSHIP

★Denotes amateurs

Name	Scores				Total	Money
Greg Norman, Australia	74	63	74	69	280	£70,000
Gordon J. Brand, England	71	68	75	71	285	50,000
Bernhard Langer, West Germany	72	70	76	68	286	35,000
Ian Woosnam, Wales	70	74	70	72	286	35,000
Nick Faldo, England	71	70	76	70	287	25,000
Seve Ballesteros, Spain	76	75	73	64	288	22,000
Gary Koch, USA	73	72	72	71	288	22,000
Fuzzy Zoeller, USA	75	73	72	69	289	17,333
Brian Marchbank, Scotland	78	70	72	69	289	17,333
Tsuneyuki Nakajima, Japan	74	67	71	77	289	17,333
Christy O'Connor Jr, Ireland	75	71	75	69	290	14,000
David Graham, Australia	75	73	70	72	290	14,000
Jose-Maria Canizares, Spain	76	68	73	73	290	14,000
Curtis Strange, USA	79	69	74	69	291	11,500
Andy Bean, USA	74	73	73	71	291	11,500
Anders Forsbrand, Sweden	71	73	77	71	292	9,000
Jose-Maria Olazabal, Spain	78	69	72	73	292	9,000
Raymond Floyd, USA	78	67	73	74	292	9,000
Bob Charles, New Zealand	76	72	73	72	293	7,250
Manuel Pinero, Spain	78	71	70	74	293	7,250
Ronan Rafferty, N. Ireland	75	74	75	70	294	5,022
Derrick Cooper, England	72	79	72	71	294	5,022
Vaughan Somers, Australia	73	77	72	72	294	5,022
Ben Crenshaw, USA	77	69	75	73	294	5,022
Robert Lee, England	71	75	75	73	294	5,022
Philip Parkin, Wales	78	70	72	74	294	5,022
Danny Edwards, USA	77	73	70	74	294	5,022
Vicente Fernandez, Argentina	78	70	71	75	294	5,022
Sam Torrance, Scotland	78	69	71	76	294	5,022
Ian Stanley, Australia	72	74	78	71	295	3,800
John Mahaffey, USA	75	73	75	72	295	3,800
Masahiro Kuramoto, Japan	77	73	73	72	295	3,800
D.A. Weibring, USA	75	70	76	74	295	3,800
Sandy Lyle, Scotland	78	73	70	74	295	3,800
Tom Watson, USA	77	71	77	71	296	3,168
Roger Chapman, England	74	71	78	73	296	3,168
Andrew Brooks, Scotland	72	73	77	74	296	3,168
Ron Commans, USA	72	77	73	74	296	3,168
Mark James, England	75	73	73	75	296	3,168
Payne Stewart, USA	76	69	75	76	296	3,168
Gary Player, South Africa	75	72	73	76	296	3,168
Gregory Turner, New Zealand	73	71	75	77	296	3,168
Roger Maltbie, USA	78	71	76	72	297	2,800
Mark O'Meara, USA	80	69	74	74	297	2,800
Ho Ming Chung, Taiwan	77	74	69	77	297	2,800
Mac O'Grady, USA	76	75	77	70	298	2,475
Jack Nicklaus, USA	78	73	76	71	298	2,475
Tony Charnley, England	77	73	76	72	298	2,475
Fred Couples, USA	78	73	75	72	298	2,475
Michael Clayton, Australia	76	74	75	73	298	2,475
Larry Mize, USA	79	69	75	75	298	2,475
Jeff Hawkes, South Africa	78	73	72	75	298	2,475

Lu Hsi Chuen, Taiwan	80	69	73	76	298	2,475
Bob Tway, USA	74	71	76	77	298	2,475
Tommy Armour III, USA	76	70	75	77	298	2,475
Sam Randolph, USA	72	76	77	75	300	2,150
Graham Marsh, Australia	79	71	75	75	300	2,150
Carl Mason, England	76	73	73	78	300	2,150
Mark McNulty, South Africa	80	71	79	71	301	1,925
Malcolm Mackenzie, England	79	70	77	75	301	1,925
Lee Trevino, USA	80	71	75	75	301	1,925
Eamonn Darcy, Ireland	76	75	75	75	301	1,925
Tom Lamore, USA	76	71	77	77	301	1,925
Frank Nobilo, New Zealand	76	75	71	79	301	1,925
Andrew Chandler, England	78	72	78	74	302	1,650
James Heggarty, N. Ireland	75	72	80	75	302	1,650
Martin Gray, Scotland	75	76	76	75	302	1,650
Donnie Hammond, USA	74	71	79	78	302	1,650
Scott Simpson, USA	78	71	75	78	302	1,650
Ossie Moore, Australia	76	74	79	74	303	1,500
Peter Fowler, Australia	80	71	77	75	303	1,500
David Jones, N. Ireland	75	76	79	75	305	1,500
Ross Drummond, Scotland	76	74	77	78	305	1,500
Tommy Horton, England	77	73	82	74	306	1,500
Gary Weir, Scotland	78	69	80	80	307	1,500
Kristen Moe, USA	76	74	82	82	314	1,500
Hubert Green, USA	77	73	81	Ret'd	—	1,500

Non-Qualifiers After 36 Holes
(All professionals receive £400)

Bill Rogers, USA	80	72	152	Paul Way, England	79 77	156
Scott Verplank, USA	77	75	152	John Bland, South Africa	82 74	156
Tom Kite, USA	78	74	152	Larry Nelson, USA	81 75	156
David Frost, South Africa	78	74	152	Denis Durnian, England	78 78	156
Neil Hansen, England	77	75	152	★ Mark Davis, England	78 78	156
Johnny Miller, USA	75	77	152	Michel Tapia, France	78 78	156
Ove Sellberg, Sweden	76	76	152	Jose Rivero, Spain	81 75	156
Peter Jacobsen, USA	77	75	152	Jim Thorpe, USA	77 79	156
Simon Bishop, England	79	73	152	Bruce Zabriski, USA	77 79	156
Philip Walton, Ireland	75	77	152	Fulton Allem, South Africa	82 74	156
Edward Webber, Zimbabwe	77	76	153	Wayne Westner, South Africa	78 78	156
Mark Mouland, Wales	77	76	153	Eddie Polland, Ireland	79 77	156
Andrew Oldcorn, England	80	73	153	Jeff Hall, England	80 77	157
Deane Beman, USA	75	78	153	Corey Pavin, USA	81 76	157
Dan Pohl, USA	75	78	153	Michael Cahill, Australia	83 74	157
Joey Sindelar, USA	80	73	153	★ Andrew Cotton, England	79 79	158
Denis Watson, South Africa	78	75	153	Seiichi Kanai, Japan	87 71	158
Des Smyth, Ireland	80	73	153	Bill Longmuir, Scotland	83 76	159
Antonio Garrido, Spain	77	76	153	Gordon Brand, Scotland	80 79	159
Martin Poxon, England	79	74	153	Glenn Ralph, England	81 79	160
David Williams, England	81	72	153	Tony Johnstone, Zimbabwe	87 73	160
David Russell, England	81	73	154	Garth McGimpsey, N. Ireland	85 76	161
Jerry Anderson, Canada	81	73	154	Ken Brown, England	81 80	161
Peter Allan, England	83	71	154	David Feherty, N. Ireland	81 80	161
Emmanuel Dussart, France	78	76	154	Paul Carrigill, England	85 76	161
Richard Masters, England	73	81	154	Adan Sowa, Argentina	86 75	161
Maurice Bembridge, England	76	78	154	Andrew Murray, Scotland	83 78	161
Peter Senior, Australia	81	73	154	★ Jeremy Robinson, England	83 79	162
Howard Clark, England	81	73	154	Robert Richardson, South Africa	85 77	162
Richard Boxall, England	78	76	154	Ray Stewart, Canada	85 79	164
Peter Teravainen, USA	75	79	154	★ David Curry, England	85 80	165
Adam Hunter, Scotland	78	77	155	Jaime Gonzalez, Brazil	85 82	167
Rodger Davis, Australia	81	74	155	Howard Francis, England	85 82	167
Terry Gale, Australia	81	74	155	Mark Wiltshire, South Africa	85 84	169
Hugh Baiocchi, South Africa	81	74	155	George Ritchie, Scotland	87 84	171
Ian Baker-Finch, Australia	86	69	155	Guy McQuitty, England	95 87	182
David Llewellyn, Wales	82	73	155	Craig Stadler, USA	82	Ret'd
Mike Harwood, Australia	77	78	155	Andrew Broadway, England		Ret'd

ROUND TURNBERRY AILSA

No. 1 350 Yards Par 4 One of the less severe opening holes in championship golf. Downwind, it leaves little more than a wedge for the second shot but, in wind from the sea, it is unwise to skirmish with the bunkers on the right of the fairway. The left side is the place to be in order to open up the green.

No. 2 428 Yards Par 4 No great definition attached to the drive except that the fairway drops away sharply to the left. Two bunkers on the approach to the green are less likely to be a hazard in an Open than they are to the average visitor. They do have an effect in distorting judgement on the second shot but, to professionals, who have every inch of the course charted, that is also less of a problem.

No. 3 462 Yards Par 4 An inviting drive down a gentle valley – again with no fairway bunkers to bar the way. However, only a long drive down the left offers a full view of the green which is well guarded on the right. At the twenty-first hole in a famous match in the Amateur of 1961, Joe Carr got a birdie to defeat Charlie Green.

No. 4 167 Yards Par 3 One of Turnberry's gems. Rather like the short fourteenth at Pine Valley; if you are not on the green, forget it. A one-shot hole that has been stretched a little over the years. The seas used to come up to the bottom of the bank on the left of the green but there have been one or two minor alterations to the green since 1977. It is a little larger and the shoulder on the right is not so pronounced.

No. 5 441 Yards Par 4 Converted from a par five to a long four for the purposes of an Open. The best line from the tee is down the right. It gives a better angle for the second shot which has to negotiate a cluster of greenside bunkers on the left. Its name "Fin' me Oot," may have meaning even in a major championship.

No. 6 222 Yards Par 3 Very much a hole where power is an asset. Can be as much as a driver but an uphill approach to the green can knock the sting out of any shot and one of the deeper bunkers sees plenty of traffic on the right. Under normal circumstances, a new view of Ailsa Craig has been opened up by the removal of the dunes.

No. 7 528 Yards Par 5 Major surgery to the dunes two winters ago now gives a superb vantage point for the sixth green and for the drives at the dogleg seventh, the only par five on the outward half. Conditions dictate the problems and the decisions on the tee. It can be a full, mighty hit or a more conservative shot downwind, perhaps even an attempt to cut the corner. There is a gambling element about the hole which boasts rough country to the left. The approach to the green consists of a long, gradual slope.

No. 8 427 Yards Par 4 The beginning of the magnificent coastal stretch. The drive has to avoid a large bunker on the right but the second shot holds the key. A well guarded, elevated green can be a difficult target with the putting surface on two distinct levels. There is the added danger of a hooked shot finishing on the beach.

No. 9 455 Yards Par 4 Vintage Turnberry, although the famous back tee on the rocks was not designed by Mackenzie Ross. It was added later by Jimmy Alexander, architect of the Arran course. The drive is less daunting for competitors in an Open but is still quite an achievement to hit the fairway. The angling of the green makes the second shot tricky.

No. 10 452 Yards Par 4 More than most holes at Turnberry, one influenced by wind strength and direction. Can be a drive and a wedge or two full woods. There is a need to err to the right rather than the left but the large central bunker short of the green is only really a hazard in a headwind or for those trying to be too ambitious with their seconds from the rough.

No. 11 177 Yards Par 3 Another tee position close to the shore. The tee itself has been much enlarged since the last Open but, otherwise, the demands are the same. With the pin tucked in on the left, the option is for a direct shot over the bunker or one played into the gap.

No. 12 441 Yards Par 4 Purchase of the land round the rocky headland has allowed this hole to be stretched by about thirty yards and provided far greater spectator access in what was a tight corner. The extra yardage has brought the fairway bunkers far more into play and given added difficulty to the second shot.

No. 13 411 Yards Par 4 As in 1977, the tee being used is the normal ladies tee on the tenth. This accentuates the dogleg of bunker and grassy hollow on the right. The ideal is to play for the gap unless players are long enough to carry all the trouble. The problem thereafter is judging the shot to a raised green with no bunkers for guidance.

No. 14 440 Yards Par 4 Probably the hardest of the par fours in the prevailing wind. The fairway is slightly hidden from the tee but the drive wants to be as far right as possible to take advantage of the narrow entrance to the green.

No. 15 209 Yards Par 3 A dramatic short hole reminiscent of the fourteenth of Royal Portrush known as Calamity Corner. A steep, grassy dell to the right but well bunkered on the left. Not an easy target. However, it was here on the final day in 1977 that Tom Watson holed a long, long putt from the left edge of the green for a two that enabled him to draw level with Jack Nicklaus.

No. 16 409 Yards Par 4 A hole that played a major part in deciding the Walker Cup in 1963. Wilson's burn encircling the front of the green is the main feature but clearance of it involves pin-point accuracy to get a position close to the flag. The banks at the back of the green and rough country beyond penalise the overstrong. The percentage shot is usually much in evidence but it is advisable first to hit the fairway from the tee.

No. 17 500 Yards Par 5 The second par five through a valley hidden from the tee but essential to hit the fairway if the narrow waist dominating the second shot is to be negotiated safely. Not as formidable a hole as, say, the seventeenth at St. Andrews but it claims its victims.

No. 18 431 Yards Par 4 Use of the 18th tee on the Arran makes this a sharp dogleg for the Open. Bunkers and out of bounds to the left push players to the right although a line of gorse hovers with which Jack Nicklaus mingled on the seventy-second hole in 1977. No bunkers surrounding the green but their absence can hamper judgement.

THE VENUE
A National Golfing Monument

By Donald Steel

Towards the end of the last century, Scottish landowners, particularly the nobility among them, were more likely to have sought their sporting pleasures from river bank, glen or moor than from the golf links which, even then, were dotted in fair profusion round their coastline. The Marquis of Ailsa was a notable exception and for the good of Turnberry, British golf and, more recently, the Open Championship, it was as well that he was.

He might also have earned an approving nod from modern owners of stately homes who have had to develop increasingly commercial instincts in order to keep the wolf from their illustrious doors. By joining forces with the Glasgow and South West Railway, the Marquis gave rise to the first purpose-planned golfing resort centre in Britain.

The first thing this entailed was for the railway company to extend the line from Ayr to Girvan and then build a station and hotel, a more logical sequence of events than in the 1960s when British Railways planned a new hotel in St. Andrews and promptly closed the branch line from Leuchars. However, of all the many people who deserve credit for guiding Turnberry's star in the early days, rescuing it after the last war when all seemed lost, and masterminding its finest hour in 1977, the Marquis was the first to realise its potential.

This was no surprise or accident since golf had been in his family's blood for many years

before that. In his wonderful book, *A History of Golf* (J.M. Dent and Sons Ltd.), Robert Browning sketched an early branch of the family tree by pointing out that the title of Marquis of Ailsa was a relatively modern creation, the ancestors of the Kennedy family being Earls of Cassilis and Lords of Culzean.

In making reference to chole, a game in which both sides played the same ball and were perfectly entitled to hit it – intentionally – into some horrible spots, rather as in croquet where you can hit your opponent's ball into the flower bed, he made the general point that sinister subterfuge was less likely to happen at golf. But he did instance an occasion to the contrary in which an ancestor of the Marquis of Ailsa played a match on "the linkes atte Air" against a monk of Crossragruel, the stake on the result being the monk's nose.

Browning went on to say that "if there is any foundation for the story, the match was probably part of the campaign of intimidation by which the then Earl of Cassilis in 1570 forced Allan Stewart, commendator of the abbey of Crossragruel, to sign a conveyance of the abbey lands to the earl."

"The luckless commendator, who was somehow prevailed upon to visit the earl at Culzean, was later conveyed to a lonely tower called the Black Vault of Dunure (the ruins of which still stand), and there roasted over a slow fire until he agreed to sign the deeds."

More than three centuries later, the Marquis of Ailsa had no need to resort to such methods in order to become captain of Prestwick Golf Club in 1899. He was elected by popular acclaim as a golfer of some ability, conscious of the part his Club had played in starting the Open Championship and in running it, first on an individual basis, and then in tandem, until such time as the Royal and Ancient took ultimate control.

The Marquis no doubt witnessed some of the early Opens which may have strengthened his motive for wanting his own course, although it may equally have stemmed from a desire not to have to travel so far for his golf; in those days, the journey to Prestwick, even with coach and four, must have been quite an undertaking.

On the other hand, he knew better than anyone the glories of Turnberry's setting and perhaps felt that that alone was a strong marketing force. Subsequently, the nearest equivalent to Turnberry in terms of setting, proved to be Pebble Beach – with which it is often compared. There, Sam Morse assumed command of Del Monte Properties and established a veritable gold mine.

All Turnberry lacked in those early days was the proper communication, a void which the Marquis filled by his agreement with the railways. By 1906, the station and hotel had opened and a frequent and fast train service from Glasgow established together with a direct sleeper service from London. This had the obvious merit of the carriages being unhooked in a siding at Turnberry, the occupants strolling, when the spirit moved them, along a covered way to the hotel for breakfast.

Not that the building of the railway was entirely free from opposition. *The Scotsman* newspaper of June 3rd 1903, reported "there are navvies now, gangs of them, defacing the fair face of Carrick along a route where Carrick looks across to Arran, to Ailsa Craig, to the outer gates of Clyde. They are making a new line of railway that is to carry the traveller through the country of the Kennedys and the heart of the land of Burns."

Reaction to change was no different then than it is now, or the speed with which criticism can become muted. On May 17th 1906, the *Glasgow Herald* covered the inauguration of the Maidens and Dunure Railway which took the form of "a complimentary visit to the magnificent new hotel and golf links at Turnberry."

The entire description that followed was centred on the hotel rather than the course although the *Ayr Observer and Galloway Chronicle*, covering the same occasion a day later, talked of "being afforded the privilege of a game at golf over the splendid course laid out in 1901 by Willie Fernie."

The Fernies, Willie and George, of Troon and Dumfries, were respected pro-greenkeepers in the latter half of the 1880s and Willie was therefore the obvious candidate to submit the design for Turnberry at a time when golf course architecture had not yet become a recognised profession. The results of his labours were two courses – No. 1 measuring 6,115 yards and No. 2 5,115 yards with both open on Sundays which was as rare as a Scotsman confessing publicly to a dislike of the bagpipes or haggis.

An unusual occurrence, not to say unique, was the appointment of Tom Fernie, Willie's son, as Turnberry's first professional. To take over on a course which your father had designed had a precedent only in Young Tom Morris succeeding his father, Old Tom, as Open champion. But Turnberry's first chapter was a distressingly short one.

By 1914 and the advent of war, Turnberry was commissioned as a training centre for the Royal Flying Corps and other Commonwealth Flying Units. The flying machines of those magnificent men, among them J.B. McCuddon, who won the Victoria Cross, were mercifully light and did not require the concrete runways that scarred the landscape 25 years later although the risks of military flying, then in its infancy, is reflected in the War Memorial to the fallen which stands on the hill beside the present twelfth green.

The hotel was requisitioned for that period as an officers' mess but life quickly got back to normal and Carters of Raynes Park were soon engaged to build a new No. 2 course which became so good and popular that titles based on numerical merit were no longer appropriate. When the London Midland and Scottish Group assumed control of the Glasgow and South West railways, and took over total ownership of Turnberry from the Marquis, the now familiar names, Ailsa and Arran, were conferred on the courses but Turnberry's championship status, begun in 1912 with Gladys Ravenscroft winning the Ladies British Open Amateur, was admirably preserved with a succession of ladies championships, British and Scottish, between the wars.

The most notable was that in 1921 when Cecil Leitch inflicted on Joyce Wethered her only defeat in the final of a national championship, an event graced by the presence of Bernard Darwin who described as "memorable" the first round meeting of Leitch and Alexa Stirling, the reigning American champion from the same Club in Atlanta as Bobby Jones. Memorable in a different context was the weather for that game. Turnberry is not alone among seaside links in being heaven or hell – often in the same day – and Darwin revealed years later how the dripping notes he tried to keep provided as vivid a memory as the golf he had faithfully followed.

Quite why the men were so reluctant to extend their patronage for championships is one of the more major mysteries. It is true that Scotland has always been rich in the number of its championship venues, not all so welcoming to women, but Turnberry was conscious that there were improvements to be made. Consequently, Major Cecil Hutchison, a well known name in golf course architecture who had had a hand in shaping Gleneagles, was called in.

It was no doubt that his work there prompted his invitation to try and boost the Ailsa's popularity by eliminating some of the blind shots and introducing more length, a task completed in 1938 which earned the commendation of Darwin.

Had Hitler's wickedness been supressed in the 1930s, it is possible that Hutchison's work would have been further hailed as fit for an Open but no sooner had it been unveiled, than heavy dust covers were laid over it, so to speak. Its subsequent destruction was as devastating as if the art treasures of Florence had been lost in a fire or the Mona Lisa the target of vandals.

Turnberry's geographical position was thought to be of such strategic importance that its conversion a second time by the War Office was ordered. Many other of our great links suffered to the extent of being defended by pill boxes, mines and barbed wire to make invasion more difficult, some like Prince's with lasting consequences. The post-war Prince's has never hosted an Open, as the first did in 1932, but at least it survived.

Turnberry's very existence was threatened; and that for a small town or village that lived for its golf and because of its golf was verging on calamity. Commandeered by RAF Coastal Command, fairways, bunkers, tees and greens were flattened by insensitive bulldozers and converted by concrete mixers to landing strips capable of handling the Liberators and Beaufighters so essential to the spotting of German U-boats.

Training for this involved a lot of low flying over the Firth of Clyde with more than the odd casualty, a state of affairs that led seasoned fliers to question the suitability of Turnberry for the purpose. However, whatever the wisdom of turning it into an airfield, it didn't alter the desolation that faced those with the responsibility of picking up the pieces in 1946.

Many of the hotel directors, on surveying the scene, felt like running up the white flag from its masthead. They saw no future, but one man who did was Frank Hole, Chairman of British Transport Hotels Ltd., as the group became with the nationalisation of the railways by Attlee's government. Hole fought Whitehall in a long and vigorous battle for financial compensation which led in 1949 to a contract at last being let to Suttons of Reading to perform the miracle of transformation of runway back to fairway.

The magic wand they waved was conjured up by Philip Mackenzie Ross who masterminded the whole operation even to the extent of building plasticine models that showed the slopes, shapes and contours he wanted. There has never been, either before or since, an operation to compare with it; nor a project where every square yard of fairway, tee and green was turfed instead of seeded.

By 1951, troubled waters were calm once more, the Ailsa course reopened and rave notices flooded in. Demand to hold tournaments and championships was enormous. It owed much to the design of Mackenzie Ross, whose modern version was an undoubted masterpiece; but the biggest effect it had on first time visitors was why they hadn't been there before. With Turnberry, seeing really is believing. It was as if a new, promised land had been discovered.

The heart of the Ailsa lies on the coastal stretch of holes from the fourth to the eleventh, a mingling of dune and rocky crag with the close proximity of the ocean. This is most apparent on the tees of the fourth, ninth and eleventh, but broader horizons encompass some of the most stunning scenery in golf's firmament.

My own introduction came in the Amateur

Championship of 1961 and I don't remember being more moved by the first sight of any course or, more accurately, the course and the splendours of its surroundings as seen from the terrace of the hotel. It was a morning when the full panoply was unfurled. The peaks of Arran, the Mull of Kintyre and the sunlit waters lapping Ailsa Craig whose reputation for providing the finest curling stones was always well plugged on television by Henry Longhurst.

Turnberry's sterner moods are exemplified by the day in 1973 when a fierce wind blew many of the tents down in the John Player Classic and on the first day of the 1986 Open which may have been some revenge for the relative peace and quiet of 1977. With any seaside links, you learn to take the rough with the smooth, but it wasn't just the likelihood of a brisk wind to stiffen the defences of the Ailsa that boosted its reputation.

Its graduation to the highest ranks was dazzlingly swift, an eminence that was doubly justified by the quality of the champions it produced. Michael Bonallack used the 1961 Amateur as a launching pad to the greatest record since the faraway days of John Ball; Christy O'Connor, Eric Brown and David Thomas were as worthy matchplay champions as the PGA or the News of the World could have found; Sandy Lyle landed the European Open in the best manner possible in 1979, a final round of 65; Philip Parkin won the 1983 Amateur as easily as any one could have done; and no finer compliment could have been paid than when Tom Watson and Jack Nicklaus made the 1977 Open their very own.

It took the crowning glory of that Open to complete a romantic tale that tells of so much change, upheaval and earnest faith. It is important for each new generation of golfer to be reminded of this because historical records can soon be lost, particularly such detail as the loss of the railway from the hotel's back door.

However, as vivid a memory of Turnberry as any for me took the form of the Braemar tournament in 1964, which was a fully-fledged PGA tournament with the novel variation that the number of clubs a player was permitted to carry, or have carried, was limited to seven.

Apart from appealing to the traditionalists who believe that the game has been made harder, not easier, by being allowed fourteen clubs – never mind the effect it has had on the speed of play – it encourages the strokemaker

and not those stereotyped golfers who treat every shot the same. Lionel Platts' winning score in far from easy conditions was 288 although Turnberry, in most normal circumstances, has never denied success or a spectacular score to those who earn it.

There is no trickery or deceit. The problems, if difficult, are natural and all plain to see – the hallmark of a great architect. Mackenzie Ross struck the perfect balance between what is challenging and what is unfair. There is frequently a thin dividing line, but it was the amateurs as much as the professionals who gave the Ailsa course the recognition necessary to its rapid climb up the charts once its rehabilitation period was over.

In the sadly defunct match between Amateurs and Professionals in 1958, it was the amateurs who handed out a lesson to the masters; two of the most notable results were the defeats of Eric Brown and Christy O'Connor by Joe Carr and Reid Jack. However, following the Home Internationals in 1960, the blue riband came with the staging of the Walker Cup in 1963.

There were hopes, too, of a home victory at the start of the second day. The American team that included Deane Beman, Billy Joe Patton and Charlie Coe were behind by 7½ matches to 4½ and wearing a distinctly worried look, but on the Saturday morning all four foursomes slipped away from the British and Irish, two of them through calamities on the sixteenth, and the afternoon brought no trace of a revival.

The next few years brought limelight in the form of countless pro-ams and pro-celebrity televised matches which introduced millions to the scenic delights now familiar to those understandably tempted to go and see for themselves. To set the domestic record straight, the last chapter in the story of Turnberry came when Margaret Thatcher's government sold the railway hotels as part of their privatisation scheme and Seaco, later called Venice-Simplon Orient-Express Hotels became the new owners.

Thus ended an eighty-year connection with the railways, but an insistence upon redoubling the search for excellence regarding all aspects of Turnberry was indicative of how highly they rate the asset value of their new possession. It is nothing short of a national golfing monument.

The Turnberry Hotel opened in 1906 and trains from Glasgow, along with a direct sleeper service from London, enabled visitors easy access to the golf course designed by Willie and George Fernie

Scenes from Turnberry Hotel (above) and Culzean Castle (below), four miles from Turnberry (Photographs copyright Ronny Jacques/GOURMET)

Burns Cottage (above), birthplace of Robert Burns in Alloway, and the gardens at Turnberry Hotel (below)

RETROSPECTIVE
The Watson-Nicklaus Epic Of 1977

By Donald Steel

One advantage of having had 114 Open championships is that there is plenty of scope for reminiscence. When reviewers consider the battles fought over our old established links like St. Andrews or Muirfield, they have no difficulty striking a nice balance between ancient and modern.

To the romantic beginnings of Old and Young Tom, they add a rich helping of Vardon, Taylor and Braid; a generous measure of Jones and Hagen; a liberal sprinkling of Snead, Locke, Thomson and Palmer; and, finally, coming right up to date, they indulge in colourful portrayals of current heroes. It is as hard deciding whom to leave out as whom to put in.

With Turnberry, there is no such problem. Until 1986, when you have dealt with Tom Watson and Jack Nicklaus in 1977, you have said it all. The latest of the courses used for the Open, and the last addition to the rota in the forseeable future, perhaps ever, its Open Championship "traditions" are more instant; but however deep historians delve into the record books, it is impossible to believe that, for sustained brilliance and drama, anything ever exceeded those four sunlit days on Turnberry's great Ailsa course. Beginner's luck or divine intervention, there were times when it seemed more fiction than fact.

For one thing, the two central figures were the two finest players in the world at that time. Since the days of the Triumvirate, it is rare how often that has happened. The second thing which set 1977 apart was the way that Watson and Nicklaus ran right away from the rest of the field. They might almost have been playing a different course. While they shattered the record aggregate for the Open, Watson by eight strokes and Nicklaus by seven, only one other player, Hubert Green, beat par for the four rounds and then by only a single stroke. Eleven strokes behind Watson, Green never spoke a truer word in saying, "I won the other tournament."

An examination of the reasons for such unparalleled scoring lies as much as anything in the benign weather. In the John Player Classic of 1973, the wind blew so savagely that it made golf a battle for survival. Even Watson or Nicklaus would have been looking to break 80 rather than 70 but four years later the chief meteorological interruption was a thunderstorm on Friday which had the two leaders sheltering on the beach out by the tenth hole. It merely cleared the air from one settled, warm spell and paved the way for another.

In their peaceful moods, seaside links can be ripe for the picking of low scores although Watson and Nicklaus began relatively modestly in view of what was to follow. The early spotlight fell on two less celebrated Americans in a championship which turned out to be totally dominated by Americans. They claimed eleven of the first twelve places.

There is an inborn fear among golf writers that the leader will come from the last match on a long first day and that is exactly what occurred. Carefully researched stories were torn up and headlines rewritten as John Schroeder, son of Frank, the 1949 Wimbledon champion, returned a 66, but part of that inborn fear of the Press is based on a reluctance to overdo the billing on the grounds that first round leaders have a habit of disappearing as fast as they emerge. Schroeder ran true to form.

His lead was taken over on Thursday by Roger Maltbie, playing in his first Open, whose 66, added to an opening 71, took him one stroke ahead of Nicklaus, Watson, Green and Trevino. In his cross examination that followed, Maltbie endeared himself to the Scottish section of the Press by revealing that his mother came from Kirkintilloch although his main surprise about the course was there wasn't a tree to be seen on it.

Ballesteros, who had made such a notable impression the year before at Birkdale, was challenging promisingly at one stage on the second day, but the unsuspecting center of attention was Mark Hayes. Under a white, floppy sun hat, he put together the most spectacular round, statistically at any rate, in the whole history of the Open, a 63 that beat Henry Cotton's long held record of 65 at Sandwich in 1934.

I still remember the surprise I felt that the Ailsa course, one of the most noble of our links, had been caught so defenceless by a player hardly cast in the heroic mould. It was a terrible blow to its dignity but the round might so easily have been a stroke less. Converted to a cross-handed putting method only a week or so earlier, Hayes stood on the eighteenth needing a four for a 62, but the uneasy five he took largely by trying to cut the corner and bunkering his drive, indicated his sudden awareness and subsequent apprehension that accompanied his date with destiny.

Green was another who might have matched Hayes until the putts started to run out on him; but the significant development, largely unsung and unnoticed, was the way Watson and Nicklaus had slipped into the picture. Their rounds of 68 and 70 may have lacked the individual glamour so apparent on the first two days but the Derby isn't won in the first half mile at Epsom. You just need to be well positioned and ready and able to pounce. That described Watson and Nicklaus nicely.

The real buzz of excitement came when the draw for the third day announced that they had been paired together, not only because most saw one or other of them as the likely winner, but because three months earlier at Augusta, Watson had won the Masters by two strokes from Nicklaus, a victory of vital importance to him in his quest to becoming a great championship winner. Turnberry was his chance to show it was no fluke. For Nicklaus, there was nothing left to prove except his astonishing capacity for enduring consistency unmatched in championship golf. For twenty-five years, he has been the yardstick by which others can judge their progress and performance.

It didn't take long for the sparks to fly in the third round and for the pair of them to spell out the message that everyone else was wasting his time thinking of victory although Palmer, a few weeks short of his forty-eighth birthday, and Peter Thomson reminded the large crowd that there were other great champions around. They had scores of 67.

Nicklaus, with birdies at the second and fourth, went three ahead after four holes, Watson replying with a birdie at the fifth but unable to match Nicklaus's two at the sixth or his outward half of 31 despite further birdies at the seventh and eighth. It was at this point that the storm called a temporary halt to proceedings but, if the celestial fireworks passed, the terrestrial ones did not.

Nicklaus, with the chance of a three-stroke lead on the fourteenth, went a little too strongly for his first putt and missed the return; but Watson's two at the fifteenth was a telling thrust in an inward half of 32 which saw the two of them level again with a round to play. Their rounds of 65 maintained the symmetry of their scoring following identical rounds of 70 and 68; what is more, they set a new fifty-four-hole record aggregate of 203 – one that remained until Watson lowered it by a stroke at Muirfield in 1980.

It was all a case of Nicklaus and Watson bringing the best out in each other, but it did not seem possible that they could maintain such a standard or continue playing virtually stroke for stroke – as they had done from the start. However, in a sense, the championship was only just beginning.

In the Interview Room at Augusta the previous April when Nicklaus was being asked whether something which a leading player had said about him ("We're not as scared of him as we used to be") had had anything to do with his final 66, Watson, waiting his turn at the microphone, stepped forward.

"Let me say something about that," he said, "I am always afraid of this man." "No he's not," said Nicklaus smiling, "he's not afraid of anybody. That's why he won."

Their ability to sustain the longest spell of brilliance in the Open since Henry Cotton in 1934 was generated more out of respect for each other than fear, plus the built-in quality of any great, natural competitors never to acknowledge defeat. For the second day running, Nicklaus opened the final round with two birdies in the first four holes which took him three ahead of Watson who dropped a stroke at the second.

Watson's second consecutive three at the fifth heralded a definite revival of spirits and he gained another stroke at the par-five seventh where he was well home in two and then drew level with yet another birdie at the eighth. It was at this point that some reinforcement of the crowd marshalling was requested by the players and there was a delay while more recruits were summoned. On the resumption, Watson took five at the ninth to be out in 34 to Nicklaus's 33 and a few holes later Nicklaus was nine strokes ahead of everyone except his partner.

The three holes from the turn were crucial for although Nicklaus increased his lead to two strokes with a three at the twelfth, thanks to a putt of six yards after driving into the rough, he had missed two holeable birdie putts on the tenth and eleventh. Watson, on the other hand, short of the tenth and twelfth in two and bunkered at the short eleventh, had to work desparately hard in order to save his pars at all three.

As they stood on the thirteenth tee, therefore there must have been widely contrasting thoughts in their minds, Watson that he was thankful not to be further behind and Nicklaus that, given a slightly different roll of the dice, all would have been as good as over. Nevertheless, the question remaining to be answered was whether Watson could give Nicklaus two strokes and overtake him in six holes.

Most were doubtful, even those with money on Watson, but he came again with a birdie at the fourteenth and then delivered the first of his subsequent body blows by holing a long putt for a two from off the fifteenth green after

his tee shot had been a little fortunate to miss the two bunkers on the left. Had it been a match, which, in effect, it was, the pattern of the previous hour or so would have suggested that the emphasis had shifted, but it is easier to see and say that in hindsight.

It was becoming like one of the old Western films when the outcome rested on the gunfighter whose ammunition lasted longest and the seventeenth brought ominous signs for Nicklaus. After Watson had hit the green with a long iron, Nicklaus was shaken enough to miss it with a four iron. His deft pitch gave him the opportunity to redeem himself but he missed from four feet. He was behind for the first time in two days.

All the same, with his powder running dry, he still had one dramatic salvo to fire. Whereas Watson, with the honour, hugged the corner of the dogleg with a perfect iron, Nicklaus, reached for the driver for the first time on the eighteenth in four rounds.

As I remember Peter Thomson commenting at the time, "It was Sydney or the bush," an old Australian saying reflecting the gambler's acknowledgement that there comes a moment when you have to risk all. In Nicklaus's case, it was almost literally the bush, his ball coming to rest so close to a dense clump of gorse that it was impossible to see how he could have any worthwhile stroke, particularly as Watson had already hit a magnificent seven iron to within a couple of feet of the hole.

However, such an epic struggle could not possibly have come to a tame ending; nor did it. Nicklaus somehow managed to heave an eight iron to the front of the green whereupon he inflamed the drama by holing for a three. Bedlam ensued, relieved only when Nicklaus raised his arms for silence for Watson. It wasn't quite a mark of surrender. He has shown countless times that such a word does not feature in his vocabulary, but his courtesy to an opponent was typical of the way in which he has always played the game.

So, too, was his reaction after Watson had holed safely. In contrast to many modern tennis players who, apart from betraying the spirit of the law which used to be observed and who only have time for the briefest of handshakes at the end of matches, his congratulations were warm and extended. It had been the perfect example of golfing combat and, by his action, Nicklaus ensured that it was a championship perfect in every last detail.

FIRST ROUND RESULTS

Hole	1	2	3	4	5	6	7	8	9	10	11	12	13	14	15	16	17	18	
Par	4	4	4	3	4	3	5	4	4	4	3	4	4	4	3	4	5	4	Total
Ian Woosnam	4	5	5	3	4	4	4	6	4	3	3	4	4	3	3	4	3	4	– 70
Nick Faldo	4	5	3	3	5	4	5	4	5	4	2	5	4	5	3	3	4	3	– 71
Gordon J. Brand	4	4	4	3	4	3	5	5	3	4	3	5	4	6	3	4	4	3	– 71
Robert Lee	4	5	4	3	5	3	6	5	4	4	3	5	3	4	3	3	3	4	– 71
Anders Forsbrand	4	4	4	3	4	4	5	5	5	3	2	5	4	5	3	4	4	3	– 71
Ian Stanley	5	5	4	2	5	3	6	4	4	3	3	5	3	5	2	4	4	5	– 72
Andrew Brooks	5	5	4	3	6	3	4	5	4	5	3	3	4	5	2	3	4	4	– 72
Sam Randolph	3	4	4	4	4	4	6	5	4	4	3	4	4	4	2	4	5	4	– 72
Bernhard Langer	3	5	4	2	5	5	5	4	4	4	3	4	5	5	4	3	3	4	– 72
Ron Commans	4	6	3	3	4	3	6	6	4	5	2	4	4	5	3	3	4	3	– 72
Derrick Cooper	4	4	4	3	5	4	5	5	4	5	2	4	4	5	2	4	4	4	– 72

HOLE SUMMARY

Hole	Par	Eagles	Birdies	Pars	Bogeys	Higher	Rank	Average
1	4	1	8	92	47	5	12	4.31
2	4	0	5	49	85	14	6	4.71
3	4	0	9	81	54	9	9	4.41
4	3	0	20	95	34	4	15	3.14
5	4	0	1	51	74	27	4	4.85
6	3	0	3	52	75	23	2	3.80
7	5	0	17	78	51	7	13	5.35
8	4	0	1	31	90	31	3	5.03
9	4	0	7	67	63	16	8	4.58
Out	35	1	71	596	573	136		40.18
10	4	0	9	60	63	21	7	4.65
11	3	0	23	94	32	3	17	3.10
12	4	0	1	64	67	20	5	4.73
13	4	0	6	92	45	9	10	4.38
14	4	0	1	33	75	43	1	5.14
15	3	0	14	89	47	2	11	3.25
16	4	0	24	88	25	15	14	4.22
17	5	7	96	38	10	1	18	4.36
18	4	0	15	100	33	4	16	4.18
In	35	7	189	658	397	118		38.01
Total	70	8	260	1254	970	254		78.19

LOW SCORES

Low First Nine	Gordon Brand	35
	Donnie Hammond	35
	Greg Norman	35
Low Second Nine	Ian Woosnam	31
Low Round	Ian Woosnam	70

Players Below Par 0
Players At Par 1
Players Above Par 151

THE FIRST DAY
A Cold and Windy Start

By Michael Williams

There was an air of suspicion in the days'leading up to the Open Championship. It was too calm. Scarcely a breath of wind stirred the flags and as a fishing smack nosed slowly back towards Girvan harbour so it tore a crack, as if across a mirror. There was some talk of the rough, which was deep and tangled. There were the odd mutterings about the limited width of the fairways, between twenty-five and thirty yards, which may not be all that narrow but seems so when the fairway bends in the driving area. Generally however one had seldom heard so much praise for the conditioning of an Open Championship course. "Never better" seemed the concensus.

And then, on the very eve of the championship, the weather broke. A near-gale sprang up from the south and suddenly it was a whole new ball game. Players set out for the final tuning of their games in the last practice round and gave up. Others decided not to go out at all. Some said to themselves "What the hell!" and carried on. Sandy Lyle, the defending champion, was one of them. He was worth listening to afterwards.

At the eighteenth, which he had been playing with a three wood and an eight iron, he now needed two drivers. At the fifteenth, earlier perhaps a five iron to this teasing short hole, he had to hit a driver as well. At the sixteenth, where a gentle if delicately judged pitch is needed to clear Wilson's burn, he needed a one iron to be sure. At once the complaints mounted.

The rough was so savage, said Greg Norman, that he and Raymond Floyd had discussed the possibility of a player injuring himself as he tried to extricate himself. Could that player then sue the Royal and Ancient for damages? He did not know but he thought it an intriguing question. Overnight the fairways had also seemed to have come down by about ten yards in width and there were broad hints that something should be done about it.

Hurriedly Michael Bonallack, Secretary of the Royal and Ancient, was called for a Press conference. He was as unflappable and calm as one would expect of the most senior officer in golf's oldest institution. The Championship Committee still regarded the course to be fair. There was no point in cutting the semi-rough because it acted as a cushion in front of the thick rough and there was less point in doing anything with the thick rough because there would be no means of carting it away. And in any case the forecast was that the wind would not be as strong on the morrow.

What no one wanted, least of all the R&A, was a repeat of the very variable weather suffered the year before at Royal St. George's. Then the players out on the afternoon of the first day and the morning of the second had got by far the roughest deal. Lyle had been one of the lucky ones.

Often such changes of weather are dictated by the turn of the tide at high water. A telephone call to the harbourmaster at Girvan revealed that high water would be at around 8 a.m. and then again some twelve hours later. It was his opinion, as a man of the sea, that the weather, whatever it would be, would stay about the same all day.

For all that there was doubt and uncertainty in many minds as Thursday dawned. It was grey, cold and windy; not quite as windy and it had also shifted to the west. Nor were the early omens any better. Ray Stewart, out in the first group at 7.30 a.m., drove into the rough, could not play it and had to take a penalty drop. Some early red figures appeared on the leader boards but they never stayed there for long. Par began to get recognition instead. Then it became the one overs. It was that sort of day.

But there is always someone who gets it round and that man was Ian Woosnam, who last year had played his part in Europe's famous victory in the Ryder Cup. A chunky little Welshman with a stout heart, he played the inward half in 31 for a 70. He was the only man to match par though, realistically, it felt more like five under. Moreover it could be measured against an average score of 78.19.

For a long time it had looked as if Nick Faldo, who has been trying to re-build his swing for the past twelve months with only slow success, had done the trick with a 71 that he brought in soon after lunch. But Woosnam sneaked past him in the early evening and then, as a pale sun began to dip towards the Mull of Kintyre, Gordon J. Brand, Robert Lee and one of that rising crop of young Swedish golfers, Anders Forsbrand, all came in with 71s as well.

Behind them, on 72, were another five, of whom the most significant was perhaps Bernhard Langer, who had prepared for this championship as diligently as anyone. Andrew Brooks, who limits his golf these days only to Scotland, was another, together with two Americans in Ron Commans and Sam Randolph, only recently turned professional, Derrick Cooper, an Englishman, and an Australian, Ian Stanley.

It had not been the most promising of days for the Americans. Gary Koch had managed a 73 and Andy Bean, Donnie Hammond and Bob Tway 74s. Hammond had in fact started sensationally, holing his second shot to the first for an eagle and following it with a birdie at the

second. But it did not last and others never got going at all.

Jack Nicklaus took 78 and so did Raymond Floyd, which was hardly to be expected of the American Masters and Open champions. Lyle, the defending champion, kept them company and Seve Ballesteros, the clear favourite at 7-2, could do no better than a 76. No one had talked more confidently beforehand than Greg Norman and when he went out in 35 he was doing better than most. His 39 home hurt but it was not disastrous.

The odd thing about Woosnam's 70 was that there was very little sign of it for nine holes. Indeed it was the opposite when he started with bogeys at the second and third and followed with a four at the sixth, that always difficult short hole. It might even have been a five since he visited both the left rough and a bunker.

There was some cheer when he pitched to twelve feet for a four at the long seventh but a hooked drive at the next led to a six and, with an outward half of 39, the Welshman's thoughts were centred very much on trying to get around in 77 or 78. He knew others were having their troubles too.

Just as suddenly, things began to go right. Woosnam began to putt better. He holed from twelve feet for a three at the tenth, played the next two holes well and then saved par at the thirteenth. But it was without doubt the fourteenth, on the day the most difficult hole on the course, that made his round.

At 440 yards dead into wind, it was an absolute terror. All day there were only thirty-three pars from the one hundred and fifty-three players and no one, until Woosnam, managed to reach it in two. Furthermore he holed the putt for a birdie, the only one there all day, from twenty feet. "It was," he later reflected, "the best one iron I have ever hit in my life. I had watched Hubert Green take a three wood from just behind me and he finished thirty yards short."

That was the inspiration and though there was still a par to be saved at the fifteenth, from a bunker, Woosnam still had an ace card tucked up his sleeve. A drive and six iron to the seventeenth, downwind of course, left him twelve feet from the flag and in went the putt for an eagle. It was the seventh at that hole that day and against par it was the most vulnerable hole. With ninety-six birdies it came out with a playing average of 4.36. The fourteenth, conversely, averaged 5.14.

Woosnam said later that he had dreamed all his life of one day leading the Open, though of course he would rather be doing it on the last day than the first. He had also come into the championship with some back trouble but a Troon osteopath, Jan Der Fries, had helped a lot and movement was getting less and less painful.

It was as tough a day as Faldo had known, in the Open anyway. There was another the first day of the Amateur Championship at Hoylake in 1975, that he was convinced was worse. "Every par you got was great and every birdie fantastic," he reflected. When in the rough he took nothing bigger than an eight iron to get out, just to be on the safe side.

Faldo always had his eye on the seventeenth to shore up his round but it was the birdies he also made at the sixteenth and eighteenth that made all the difference. They gave him an inward half of 33 and he got a 71 which, going out, he had not thought possible.

Brand senior, as he has to be called since there is also a junior, came next with his 71 and very neat it all was too until he took six at the fourteenth. Like many another he had to hack his way through the rough before finding an ugly stance in a bunker from which he was thankful to extricate himself the first time.

Still, it did not matter too much since he finished with two birdies and, having been playing well all year, he felt confident that he could sustain his tempo, which is notable for a very deliberate pause at the top of his backswing. Then came Forsbrand, who had finished second the week before in the Car Care Plan tournament at Moortown, and finally Lee, of the 71s. Here is an engaging young man who made something of a mark at Royal St. George's in 1985 and who has gone from strength to strength since. He had two birdies and an eagle in his last six holes, the impetus having come with his birdie at the thirteenth and saving pars at the next two holes.

Langer's 72 was a good solid start but he was nevertheless irritated with himself. The night before he had experimented with a new sand wedge and thought he could get more stop on the ball. So he took it out with him and at once regretted it. He left a recovery shot in a bunker at the sixth and he could not remember the last time he had done that. Altogether he felt the club had cost him at least four strokes and, had he had a long enough throw, he might well

have cast it into the waters of the Firth of Clyde.

Three bogeys in a row from the thirteenth had not helped either and the German described the fourteenth as "impossible"; not even two career-best drivers would have got him home in two. But just as his round seemed to be collapsing about him, so he pitched to twelve feet at the sixteenth, struck a four iron to nine yards at the seventeenth and holed both putts, the first for a birdie and the next for an eagle.

Norman had talked as confidently before the championship began as he has ever done and fielded the inevitable questions about his having thrown away great chances in two U.S. Opens and one U.S. Masters (two of them this year) with a nice smile and a shrug as if they had not mattered at all.

It was no surprise therefore to see him start with two birdies in his first three holes. This was more like it but at once he got tangled up with the long grass to the left of the sixth fairway, careered across to the other side and ended up taking three putts for a six. Normality returned and level par to the turn was good going.

But he made silly mistakes at the eleventh and twelfth, the latter of which led to another double bogey, due in the end to another three putts. There were times when he felt utterly humiliated by the weather. "We were reduced almost to nonentities, hacking along and trying not to take more than five at a par four," he said.

There was a 74 too from Tsuneyuki (Tommy) Nakajima, who was later to play a central part in the championship, but this was a day that made many a giant wilt at the knees. Nicklaus was one. He was rather down in the dumps when he took three putts on each of the first two greens but he steadied and was no worse off as he came off the eighth green.

But then came a quite disastrous run as he stumbled into five successive bogeys, immediately followed by a double-bogey six at the fourteenth and then another at the sixteenth, where he was in Wilson's burn. A score in the 80s therefore beckoned until, with a late flourish he managed to eagle at the seventeenth and birdie at the eighteenth.

If such a finish was reminiscent of that marvellous confrontation between Nicklaus and Watson in 1977, that was about all. Nicklaus was already calling it a "survival tournament"

(Americans are generally quite unable to distinguish between a championship and a tournament) and there was nothing from Watson to suggest that he was being motivated by a return to the scene of one of his most famous triumphs. He took 77 and, as has been the case more than once in his career, it was largely a case of bad driving and an equally indifferent short game. Such is hardly the best of combinations.

Watson maintained that the fairways were too narrow and the cross wind made them even harder to find. On reflection he felt that he had used his driver too often but learned from Brand, who used his more sparingly. The American's putting also disappointed him. If it had been better it could have been a 73, he thought; but how many golfers do not come in thinking that?

Floyd's 78 included an eight at the fourteenth and he could not remember the last time he had had one of those. The gorse bushes to the right of the fairway were quite magnetic to a number of players and when Floyd drove into them, he received a cheerful wave from some spectators that his ball had been found. In fact it was not his. Nor were three others unearthed in the same area. So back he went on the lonely trudge to the tee and proceeded to take six with his second ball.

The American champion described the conditions as bad as anything he had experienced and Ballesteros was not very happy either after his 76. What upset the Spaniard particularly was the lamentably sluggish speed of play. He claimed that it had taken him five and a half hours to get round and that, he complained, was ridiculous.

"When it is cold and windy and you have to wait, it is impossible," Ballesteros said. "We spent half an hour standing on the sixth tee,"

though there may well have been some exaggeration in that. The point he did make, which was a valid one, was that too many players are not ready to play when it is their turn. Too many players do stand around watching their partners and only "wake up" as it were after they have hit.

But the early days of an Open Championship are not only about leaders. They are also about dreams and shattered dreams. Into such a category fell Andrew Broadway. He had only been a professional for six months and this was his first Open. He had qualified most respectably at Western Gailes with two 70s. Unfortunately, however, he was suffering from some back twinges and had fixed an appointment with a physiotherapist after his round.

A consoling shoulder might have been of more help, for Broadway, 25, from Peacehaven in Sussex, had found no haven of peace in the Turnberry winds. By the tenth hole he had asked Bruce Zabriski, one of his partners, to stop marking his card. It was getting altogether too embarrassing. A succession of early bogeys were disappointing more than alarming. But then came a five at the short (supposedly short!) sixth and, much, much worse, a ten at the seventh when he began to wonder whether he might ever emerge from the rough.

Out in 49 was bad enough but when Broadway then followed with an eight at the tenth, it was altogether too much. "Tear it up," he instructed Zabriski, but he could not resist playing on, just for the fun of it. In fact he played a bit better and at least he had the experience of coming to the eighteenth and a round of applause from the grandstands. All that was missing was his name on the scoreboard. It had been taken down.

WELCOME TO THE 115th OPEN CHAMPIONSHIP

France (Emmanuel Dussart)   Australia (Rodger Davis)   Brazil (Jaime Gonzalez)

New Zealand (Greg Turner)

South Africa (Mark McNulty)

Zimbabwe (Tony Johnstone)

Argentina (Vicente Fernandez)

Taiwan (Ho Ming Chung)

Canada (Jerry Anderson)

Sweden (Anders Forsbrand)

USA (Curtis Strange)

W. Germany (Bernhard Langer)

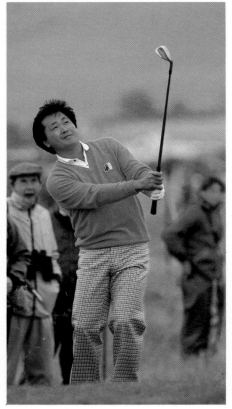

Japan (Masahiro Kuramoto)

Spain (Manuel Pinero)

Some USA contestants, including Fuzzy Zoeller, arrived via Concorde (previous page, above). Ground transportation was provided by Ford (previous page, bottom left). R&A Secretary Michael Bonallack (above left) and the official starter prepare for the first day, which saw tee times from 7.30 until 4.25

Ian Woosnam missed this birdie putt at the eighteenth but returned a level-par 70 for the lead in the first round

Gordon J. Brand was pleased with his 71

As in 1985, Robert Lee (71) was joint second

Anders Forsbrand (71) led the Swedes   Nick Faldo (71) was the first in with that score

COMMENTARY

Fickle Nature, Fickle Memories

By Mark Wilson

The memories of the world's best golfers and the ways of nature are equally fickle. In certain stressful situations they can make a volatile brew. So when Turnberry mixed the two, and did the stirring with a thirty miles-an-hour wind, trouble was inevitable. Greg Norman, the eventual winner, rated the result an intimidating, humiliating, hacking, brutal experience. He heard no arguments from the other one hundred and fifty-two challengers who toiled to limit their torture to just 1,251 shots over par for this first day of the 115th Open Championship. They were content to survive as their recollections of the course from nine years before suffered a variety of violent deaths.

Turnberry, 1977, inspired a great many misconceptions. As a newcomer to the Open rota Turnberry gained immediate immortality by producing one of the greatest, perhaps the greatest, championship of all time. Tom Watson, the winner at twelve under par, and Jack Nicklaus, second by a shot, had stretched an incredible duel to the extent of matching birdies at the seventy-second hole. The winning total of 268 set a record, as did the second-round 63 by Mark Hayes. As time passed, memories pigeon-holed Turnberry as a low-scoring venue. How wrong can you be! Turnberry made its Open debut in a drought and the rough was so sparse that even the rabbits moved away. The wind came from the less-troublesome north-east, and by Ayrshire coast standards, rarely got above the strength of a breeze. Yet only Watson, Nicklaus and Hubert Green, a faraway third on 279, finished under par. The signs were all there to heed for the return of the Open, but the world's best golfers only like to remember the good things in life. It's part of the religion they call Positive Thinking.

One look at Turnberry, 1986, was enough to jolt them back to reality. The rough was so thick and tall that the rabbits must have had awful trouble finding their way back home. The Championship Committee narrowed the fairways sufficiently to revive Lee Trevino's joke about the need to walk in single file. And, slowly but surely through the practice days, the wind mounted. In the final hours before the real action it became strong enough for Trevino to make a prophetic prediction. Scores of 80 or worse were possible, he thought, if the wind persisted. It did persist and he was among the forty-seven first-round players to take 80 or more. Norman ranked Turnberry as "probably the toughest golf course I have played for any championship." But Norman insisted that he liked the course, the tougher the better, and he hoped the wind would blow for at least two or three days. He got his wish.

Setting up a championship course is often a thankless task. Among one hundred and fifty-three players there will always be those who think the greens are too fast, those who condemn them as too slow, and others who will be critical of the narrow, wide, hard, soft fairways. Turnberry was no exception. Michael Bonallack, who mastered Turnberry well enough to make it the scene of the first of his own five Amateur Championship wins, answered for the Royal and Ancient: "Setting up a course, particularly in this country, is something fairly imprecise. You don't really say how long the rough should be because that is under the control of nature. It's not unfair. But it will be difficult. They will have to play with their heads." And with that advice, unsolicited and therefore within the rules, he stood aside for the Open to start.

The first round began at 7.30 a.m., finished close to 10 p.m., suffered a westerly wind, the most demanding, gusting up to thirty-five miles an hour, and favourite Severiano Ballesteros was made doubly unhappy by his six-over-par 76 having taken over five hours to complete. Everybody seemed to be searching everywhere for golf balls lost in the rough. Some, like the one U.S. Open champion Raymond Floyd hit at the 440-yards fourteenth, were never found. It cost him a quadruple-bogey eight and score of 78. More unfortunate on the same hole was former U.S. Masters winner Craig Stadler. The wrist he damaged playing a recovery shot became so painful that he withdrew after shooting 82. To add to the general grief, it was bitterly cold. On the tee at 8.30 a.m. to endure the worst of the conditions, Norman looked more massive than usual in layers of protective clothing that included thermal underwear and a couple of cashmere sweaters. Oh, to be in Scotland now that summer is here, they tried to whistle through gritted teeth.

More audible were the cries of anguish as the pain of chilled fingers on the tee, strained wrists in the knee-high rough, and, most of all, wounded pride everywhere, replaced the favoured memories of a sun-blessed Turnberry from 1977. Golf this day, decreed Nicklaus with all the authority of his twenty major championships, had become a game of survival. But there was nothing wrong with that, he opined. The course was the same for them all. Others, choosing to ignore this paramount fact, shifted their arguments about it being unfair on to the shoulders of the spectator. It wasn't the kind of golf he wanted to see for his money, they suggested. What a joke. Since

when did the average tournament professional care tuppence for Joe Public? To put that thought to the test – and a swift death – just propose that he be given full value for his gate money by being allowed inside the ropes, back on the fairways along with the television cameras and boom microphones.

Fortunately, the hysterics were tempered by sufficient voices of reason. The understanding and maturity of Floyd stood out. He could easily have bleated about losing a ball at the fourteenth, where the head-on wind had the green out of reach in two shots for a lot of the day. Instead, he took his punishment, joking about how he found four golf balls lost by others. "Any time I was in the rough it was penal. In the situation, a championship, wind, cold, these are the hardest conditions I have ever played in. Unfortunate, but that's the way it is." Floyd's exemplary, sporting acceptance of a cruel day stretched to the point of refusing a proferred excuse. What was the real par for the course he was asked at his post-78 conference? "The card says 70 and 70 is what it is for me and the rest," Floyd insisted. He is a good ambassador.

Floyd recognised and put into perspective what a championship is all about. It certainly isn't about target golf, pitch-and-putt stuff with mile-wide fairways and greens given the monsoon treatment every night. The Open Championship has to be the ultimate challenge of talent, mental capacity for the game, resolution and adaptability. When a thirty-five-miles-an-hour wind is howling up, down or across a twenty-four-yards fairway bordered by more hay than some farmers see at harvest time, then trying to read a yardage chart through eyes wet and running from the cold has to be nonsense. It's all "feel" – sensing that a seven iron is sufficient to cover 209 yards downwind, and having the confidence to use it.

Norman did at the short fifteenth, on the way to his starting 74 alongside Floyd in the worst of the early morning weather. "A very brutal day for golf," was his verdict with the thoughtful rider: "You can feel a non-entity out there, hacking around the rough, shooting a 74 that feels like a 64 at the finish." The strength of the wind made it always extremely difficult to control the ball, close to impossible at times, and as a result some of the best players in the world were being humiliated. It didn't matter whether you were a good tournament professional, an amateur or just a week-end hacker, you have to know where the ball is going, he said. And at cruel Turnberry this day, they couldn't be sure. The conditions created guess-work. "Today was the kind of day when you walk off the course with a headache from con-centrating and fighting the wind."

But the Open Championship is meant to be about mastering tough courses, humps and hollows, rough thick enough to punish, wind and rain. It is supposed to be an examination for all fourteen clubs in the bag while placing equal demands on power and finesse. Head-aches are the rewards for refusing to surrender and cry about the unfairness of it all. There are hundreds of "Have Fun at Happy Valley" tournaments. The Open is different. It has to be, and Norman accepted this to become champion.

The Open Championship never produces an unworthy or bad champion, a compliment that bears any amount of scrutiny. At the outset each year the object is simple enough: to create a golf course and attendant circumstances which will allow and encourage the best player in the field to win the title. The Royal and Ancient Championship Committee, whose powers of forceful authority and gentle persua-sion bow only to the whims of nature, has been incredibly successful in this respect. Golf has no greater record for sheer consistency. The start of the 1986 Open saw Ballesteros, Bern-hard Langer and Norman being recognised by the Sony Ranking as the top three golfers in the world. It was therefore as much a victory for the R&A as it was for them that they finished in the top six. Once again the objective had been achieved.

Along the way, however, there had been a multitude of suffering. The computerised scoreboards worked almost as hard as the players to keep pace with the bogeys, double bogeys and worse – 1,224 in all. The worst dis-asters came at the fourteenth, where Stadler moved his recovery shot in the rough no more than a few inches, Floyd found every ball but his own, and the average score for one hun-dred and fifty-two players – one quit before he got there – was an astounding 5.14 against a par of four. The mayhem on this hole amount-ed to one hundred and eighteen bogeys and worse. One solitary birdie, a drive, one iron and putt of twenty feet, belonged to Ian Woos-nam, and it swept him to the first day lead. The 222-yards sixth was almost as fearsome. Against the wind it frequently called for a driver. An average score of 3.80 resulted as ninety-eight players failed to make par. So much for memories of Turnberry in the sun and low scores. Langer, heading for his third successive top-three Open finish, included a double-bogey five at the sixth in his 72. "I am delighted; it could have been a lot worse," he said. How wise, how true.

The severity level adopted for the setting up of an Open course will always be a contentious issue. Given that only some twenty players approach it with a chance of winning in the first place, the vast majority have grounds to object. They naturally command a more sym-pathetic hearing when the weather turns so foul that the scoring average soars to 78.19 against a par of 70. But does that justify pleas for the R&A to rush out and widen the fair-ways to reduce the brutality, the hacking, the intimidation and the humiliation of it all? Heaven forbid. The Open is meant to separate the wheat from the chaff without any waste of time. Certainly, those who would have had this done wore egg on their faces the second day when on an untouched course Norman scored 63, only a rush of blood and three putts on the home green denying him another rec-ord. Until such times as the Royal and Ancient finds a way to control the weather, some days will be fairer than others. In the meantime there will always be those, like Ian Woosnam the first day of the 115th Open Championship, ready to prove that there is a way to conquer no matter what. And, be assured, the last day will always produce a true champion to satisfy the fickle memories of the world's best golfers and the capricious ways of nature.

SECOND ROUND RESULTS

Hole	1	2	3	4	5	6	7	8	9	10	11	12	13	14	15	16	17	18	Total		
Par	4	4	4	3	4	3	5	4	4	4	3	4	4	4	3	4	5	4	Total		
Greg Norman	4	3	3	2	5	3	3	5	4	3	2	4	4	3	3	3	4	5	– 63	– 137	
Gordon J. Brand	4	3	4	3	4	2	5	5	4	3	3	4	5	4	3	4	4	4	– 68	– 139	
Tsuneyuki Nakajima	4	4	5	2	5	4	5	4	4	4	2	3	4	4	2	3	4	4	– 67	– 141	
Nick Faldo	4	4	4	3	4	3	6	4	4	4	2	5	4	4	3	5	3	4	– 70	– 141	
Bernhard Langer	5	4	5	3	4	3	5	4	4	3	3	4	3	4	3	4	5	4	– 70	– 142	
Ian Woosnam	4	4	4	3	4	4	5	6	4	4	3	4	5	4	4	4	4	4	– 74	– 144	
Anders Forsbrand	4	5	4	3	4	3	5	4	5	4	2	5	4	3	3	6	4	5	– 73	– 144	
Gregory Turner	4	4	4	2	5	4	6	4	4	5	2	4	4	4	3	4	4	4	– 71	– 144	
Jose-Maria Canizares	4	3	5	3	4	2	4	5	5	3	2	4	4	5	3	4	4	4	– 68	– 144	

HOLE SUMMARY

Hole	Par	Eagles	Birdies	Pars	Bogeys	Higher	Rank	Average
1	4	0	17	100	34	0	13	4.11
2	4	0	10	81	52	8	6	4.40
3	4	0	16	98	31	6	11	4.18
4	3	1	32	97	18	3	17	2.93
5	4	0	5	73	60	13	4	4.54
6	3	0	10	70	61	10	1	3.48
7	5	1	34	87	29	0	15	4.95
8	4	0	4	66	69	12	2	4.61
9	4	0	6	88	53	4	7	4.37
Out	35	2	134	760	407	56		37.57
10	4	0	13	84	45	9	8	4.34
11	3	0	27	101	23	0	15	2.97
12	4	0	6	79	56	10	5	4.47
13	4	0	15	104	27	5	12	4.15
14	4	0	5	65	72	9	3	4.57
15	3	0	18	107	26	0	14	3.05
16	4	0	17	87	30	17	8	4.34
17	5	9	83	56	3	0	18	4.35
18	4	0	8	103	33	7	10	4.26
In	35	9	192	786	315	57		36.50
Total	70	11	326	1546	722	113		74.07

LOW SCORES

Players Below Par	15	Low First Nine	Greg Norman	32
Players At Par	8	Low Second Nine	Tsuneyuki Nakajima	30
Players Above Par	128	Low Round	Greg Norman	63

THE SECOND DAY
The Great White Shark Hits For 63

By Michael Williams

No one had spoken more confidently before the championship began than Greg Norman. He had come to Turnberry having taken a two-week holiday which he most certainly could afford since he was leader of the United States money list with already three tournament wins under his belt. To Norman, an Australian now living in Orlando, Florida, this was assuming ever greater importance for no man had ever in different years been top money winner in Australia (more than once), Europe (1982) and America. It was therefore all the more perplexing that he had still not won a major championship, though in all conscience he had had the opportunity. Nor was he allowed to forget, by an often merciless American media, that he had "collapsed" in a play-off for the 1984 U.S. Open, "choked" in the Masters when he had a chance of catching Jack Nicklaus and "blown" another U.S. Open only a month before when he failed to hold on to a one-stroke lead going into the final round.

Maybe because he is so used to them, Norman rides these barbs with an easy manner and a flashing smile. In fact he is ideal media material for if he cannot come up with something of interest when being quizzed, he will invent it. Once, when playing in the European Open at Sunningdale, he blamed a topped drive on a worm which popped its head out of the ground beside his ball just as he was commencing his downswing. I am not even sure that he did not say it winked as well!

For all that Norman still had to be taken as a serious contender. By chance I had watched him play a few holes of practice. Everything seemed to be going plumb centre and when he conceded that he was playing "pretty good," there was no need to question it. Norman had consulted Bruce Devlin, a fellow Australian who knows his game backwards, and had got the "go ahead." All Devlin checks in Norman is his ball position at the address for it does have a tendency to move either too far forward or, again, too far back. It was, it seems, perfect.

And so was his golf on this second day of the championship for as the wind eased so Norman, the Great White Shark as he is known in some quarters, bared his teeth and tore a 63 from the Ailsa course. It was not the first time such a score had been returned in an Open Championship but only two men had ever done it before: Mark Hayes here at Turnberry in 1977 and then by the Japanese player, Isao Aoki, at Muirfield in 1980. Norman was therefore into the record books, though he should have re-written them. Needing a par four at the last for a 62 and a new landmark in the history of the Open, he took three putts.

After all the trials and tribulations of the first day, when only Ian Woosnam matched par, it was almost ridiculous that Turnberry should yield such a score. It was still not that much of an easier day. In a field of now one hundred and fifty-one (Andrew Broadway pulled out and Craig Stadler reported injured with a damaged wrist), only fifteen players still managed to score in the 60s. Ten of them moreover had 69s, the next best to Norman being 67s from Raymond Floyd and Tsuneyuki (Tommy) Nakajima.

So it was Norman who hoisted himself to the top of the leader board, his 63, which was an eleven-stroke improvement on his opening round, making him three under par for the championship. It gave him a two-stroke lead from Gordon J. Brand, otherwise known as Brand senior, who played with splendid composure for a 68. On 139, Brand was the only other player under par.

Four strokes behind Norman came Nakajima after his 67 and Nick Faldo (70), followed by Bernhard Langer (70) another stroke away on 142 and then, on 144, a group of four – Jose-Maria Canizares, of Spain, Anders Forsbrand, of Sweden, Greg Turner, of New Zealand and Ian Woosnam, the overnight leader who had fallen back with a 74. There was therefore not a single American in the top nine. What a contrast that was to 1977 when the leading eight at the end of the championship were all American and eleven out of the top twelve.

Best placed now were Floyd, whose 67 had advanced him from equal seventy-first to equal tenth, Donnie Hammond, Gary Koch, Payne Stewart, Bob Tway and D.A. Weibring, all tied on 145 with Andrew Brooks, Roger Chapman, and an Australian, Ossie Moore. But the thirty-six-hole cut was not without its casualties and nearly some very famous ones.

The guillotine had fallen on 151 and right on that borderline were such notables as Sandy Lyle, the defending champion who had scraped home with a second round of 73, Seve Ballesteros, the favourite with another rather disappointing 75, and Jack Nicklaus, who made it only by dint of an eagle-three at the seventeenth on the way to a 73.

But out went Peter Jacobsen, the usually very consistent Tom Kite, former champions Johnny Miller and Bill Rogers, and Scott Verplank. All these Americans missed by a stroke while others who had to make an early departure were Deane Beman, who had otherwise come out of retirement with a fair degree of success, Joey Sindelar, Mark Mouland, winner of the Car Care Plan tournament the previous week, and four European Ryder Cup players in Howard Clark, Paul Way, Jose

Rivero and Ken Brown. Turnberry had indeed taken its toll.

This second day nevertheless belonged to one man and one man alone: Norman. He had in fact been a little concerned that the strong winds of Thursday might have affected his rhythm. It can happen. But from the very outset his set-up was right and his tempo, to use his own description, "fabulous." He said later that every time he stood over the ball "I knew the clubhead was going into the perfect position."

Yet he felt that the course had "played tough." There was still enough wind around, particularly for nine holes or so, to make the fairways quite difficult to find, but therein lay the key to making birdies. Only on the inward half did opportunity really beckon and it was then that he took advantage. Yet the signs had been there much earlier.

A straight-forward par at the first where, because of the angled fairway he settled for a four iron off the tee, was followed by three successive birdies. Norman hit a drive and eight iron to eighteen feet at the second, a drive and six iron to five feet at the third and then another six iron even closer at the short fourth. Each time single putts found the mark.

There was a slight lapse at the fifth, which consistently proved one of the more difficult holes, having been lengthened to 441 yards. Norman was marginally short with a five iron second and took three putts, albeit from thirty yards or so. But he made up for it almost immediately with an eagle-three at the seventh. A drive and one iron fairly whistled up the long, narrow gully and in went the putt, this time from around twenty feet. Disappointingly he was then short again with a five iron to the eighth but despite a second dropped shot was still out in 32 and right back in contention.

At once came a drive and six iron to five feet at the tenth, a nine iron almost stone dead at the eleventh and those two birdies hoisted red figures beside his name on the leader boards for the first time. All eyes were on him now and when Norman then moved to six under par for the round with a three at the fourteenth, where this time a three iron came to rest not a yard from the flag, the crowds seemed to converge on him from all directions.

Norman has long been a popular figure in Europe, it being here that he first began to expand as a world-class player. When at the sixteenth he pitched an eight iron beyond Wilson's burn to six feet or so and bottled that putt as well to go seven under, anything seemed possible. An eagle-birdie finish, which had to be "on" with the seventeenth such a vulnerable par five, would put him round in 60.

Nor did that possibility immediately diminish, as at the seventeenth Norman launched into a drive and then a five iron to lie eighteen feet away, with that putt for the eagle. The whole golf course seemed to come to a halt, holding its breath in expectation, but the ball slid by. For all that it was still a four at eighteen for a 62 or, for that matter, a birdie for a 61. It was totally unpredictable that he should manage neither. A two iron and seven iron to nine yards or so gave him a chance but the first putt was strong, the one back wide and that was a bogey-five and a 63.

Norman said that he did not know a 62 would have broken the championship record. All he was thinking on the eighteenth green was not leaving his first putt short. He simply mis-read the speed of the green, failing to notice the gradient on past the hole. When he had seen how close he was at seventeen, he was thinking very much in terms of a 60.

The first man into the interview tent that day was Jose-Maria Olazabal, a young Spaniard who has been making quite a name for himself in his first season on the European circuit. It was not however his 69 that was a matter of attention, but a presentation by Alastair Low, Chairman of the Championship Committee, to recognise Olazabal's unique distinction as an amateur when he won the British Boys, Youths and Amateur championships. Last year he had also been leading amateur in the Open at Royal St. George's, but this time the medal remained in its wrapper since no amateur qualified for the last two rounds.

A more significant appearance seemed at the time to be that of Langer, whose 70 had seemed enough to put him right up near the top of the leaderboard, since Norman was only just getting on his way. Langer even speculated that he could be leading at the end of the day and indeed it was more than another hour before Nakajima overtook him.

Langer had what he described as a rather "sleepy" start – it was soon after 8 a.m. that he drove off – and he dropped strokes at two of his first three holes. He missed the green at both the first and third. However the West German quickly settled with no further mishaps to the turn. And then, with two sub-stantial putts at the tenth and thirteenth, he pulled back both those lost shots and, with the seventeenth to come, was looking for a round in the 60s. It was an intense disappointment to him that he failed.

From a good drive, Langer could not make up his mind whether to hit a three iron or a one iron for his second. The lie was slightly uphill and at length he went for the bigger club, hoping to cut his ball into the green. But it was a poor shot, well to the right of the green and though he was still able to putt, he misjudged an intervening mound and barely made the front of the green. "I felt very bad," said Langer. "It is the easiest hole on the course."

Payne Stewart, who was runner-up a year ago at Sandwich, eighth in this year's U.S. Masters and then fourth in the U.S. Open at Shinnecock Hills, was well satisfied with his 69 for a total of 145. His most prophetic statement was that even par was going to be a good score and could even win. Having gone out in 33, Stewart dropped three shots at the tenth, fourteenth and fifteenth, but he did manage to eagle the seventeenth and hoped that at the end of the day he might be only four or five strokes behind.

However the first of the real fireworks came from Nakajima, who scarcely looks a golfer with his glasses and rather drooping shoulders. His record in Japan, where he has won more than £2 million and is rapidly becoming as famous as Jumbo Ozaki and Isao Aoki, belies all that. Nor is he exactly unknown beyond those shores, though his principal claim to fame has come with the thirteen he once took at the thirteenth in the Masters and a nine he had at the Road hole in the 1978 Open at St. Andrews. There he was on the green in two but putted into the horrid little Road bunker and took four to get out.

No such disaster overtook him in this second round at Turnberry. Far from it. Nakajima came home in 30 for his 67 and, beginning at the ninth, he had nine single putts in a row. That provided a transformation, for there was not much sign of a score in the 60s when he went through the turn in 37. But then came a whole flood of birdies: a two at the eleventh, a three at the next and then a run of two, three, four from the fifteenth with not one of them putts of less than ten feet. In between had been a pretty good "save" at the thirteenth as well. Talk about some Oriental magic with the putter!

It was the first time in a major championship that Nakajima had got himself into such serious contention and, in very passable English, he said that half of Japan would be sitting up the following night to watch him in the third round. His lead on 141 for the 36 holes was nevertheless short-lived. Hard on his heels came the elder Brand with a 68 for 139, the only man so far under par, though Norman was still to come.

For someone whose best finish of the year had been fifth in the Carrolls Irish Open, this was something of a surprise, if less so to Brand himself. He had, he said, been playing well all season and he did not take fright when he got away to another good start with two birdies in his first six holes. All through his rhythm was good and his very noticeable pause at the top of the backswing remained uninterrupted.

Both of those two early birdies were the result of good shots to the green rather than putting and his two iron to the sixth, which came to rest not much more than a yard from the flag, was the one that gave him the greatest satisfaction. Later there was another birdie at the tenth; either side of which he admittedly lapsed into bogeys at the eighth and thirteenth, but the momentum was maintained through to the seventeenth where, from a sidehill lie in the rough, he struck a majestic metal spoon to the heart of the green for the last of his birdies.

Brand deliberately avoided looking at leaderboards while another key to his performance lay in his restricted use of the driver. It was not until the seventh that he pulled the cover off it and altogether he used it only five times. He was surprised how much Tom Watson had used his and was not surprised how often it led him into trouble. Watson, with a 71 for 148, was clearly losing touch with the pacemakers.

Woosnam felt that his 74 was hardly a disaster, but admitted that he had not struck the ball anything like as well as he had in the first round. It took him seventeen holes before he managed a birdie and by then he had dropped five shots, two of them at the eighth. Bogeys at the fifteenth and seventeenth were due to his taking three putts.

More cheering news from a British point of view was a 70 from Nick Faldo, one stroke better than on Thursday. Out in 36 with a six at the seventh, he got the stroke back with a birdie at the 11th only to drop strokes at both the twelfth and sixteenth, where he hit a pitching wedge into the burn. A twenty-foot putt saved his five and encouraged him sufficiently to hole another long putt for an eagle at the seventeenth. The weakest part of his game, he felt, was his driving and instead he had resorted to the one iron for much of the time.

As only five players have ever won the British and U.S. Opens in the same year – Bobby Jones, Gene Sarazen, Ben Hogan, Lee Trevino and Tom Watson – it was good to see Floyd coming back with a 67. He did it in the company of Norman, which may have meant that not too many people noticed. But he generously said that it had been contagious to play with the Australian when in full flight.

Lyle, relieved at least to have qualified for the last two days, admitted that his golf had been scrappy but he did not regret having taken off the two weeks leading up to the Open. He was happier with his swing but felt it was proving a difficult course to attack.

Nicklaus was even more disappointed, hitting too many bad shots and then missing too many short putts. Langer observed that Nicklaus was catching the ball rather "fat" and leaving himself short too often. Ballesteros was not a happy man either. Nothing was right, he said: his driving, irons, chipping or putting. The only way he could think of improving was to change his head. "But you never know, two 65s in the next two days," he mused. Even he could have had little idea how close that would have come.

The leaderboard shows:

115th OPEN GOLF CHAMPIONSHIP
LEADER BOARD

HOLES	PAR	PLAYER	SCORE
35	−4	NORMAN	
36	+1	BRAND GJ	139
36	+1	NAKAJIMA	141
31	+2	FALDO	
36	+2	LANGER	142
28	+4	WEIBRING	
30	+4	CANIZARES	
36	+4	FORSBRAND	
36	+4	WOOSNAM	144
36	+4	TURNER	144

POSITION AFTER 35 HOLES	PLAYER	SCORE FOR ROUND
+	8 ZOELLER	+3
+	4 OCONNOR J	
+	8 FERNANDEZ	75
+	5 FLOYD	
−	10 PINERO	+2
−	4 NORMAN	

Greg Norman aimed to finish 3–3 for 60, but scored 4–5 for 63 to equal the Open Championship record

Three-times champion Jack Nicklaus made an eagle on the seventeenth to qualify on 151 for the last two days

Tsuneyuki Nakajima (67–141)

Bernhard Langer (70–142)

U.S. Open champion Raymond Floyd (67–145)

Ian Baker-Finch avoided problems such as this on the second day to equal a record for the biggest variation between rounds

Amateur champion David Curry (left) failed to qualify for the last two rounds. Guy McQuitty remained cheerful despite his 95–87

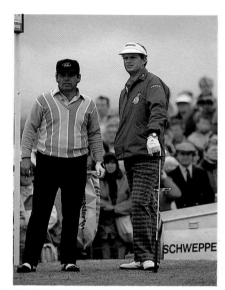

Lee Trevino and Sandy Lyle (left) were both on 151. but U.S. PGA Tour Commissioner Deane Beman (far right) lost his place

Jose-Maria Canizares's 68 lifted the Spaniard to joint sixth

COMMENTARY
Norman Lives By The Sword
By Renton Laidlaw

Few had enjoyed the first day at Turnberry. The course was set up tough for normal conditions, far less a cold, biting wind and heavy rain. The professionals had suffered and the local paper had shown a picture of Greg Norman sitting head in his hands, with the caption "Don't cry, Greg." The thirty-one-year-old Australian certainly was not crying. He had shot a 74, four off the lead on a day when no one broke par and only Ian Woosnam matched it, but he was happy with the way he played. Far from being despondent, he was really quite elated at the way things had gone. He had hit the ball well. His concentration had been good in difficult situations. He is not a negative person and his positive attitude on Thursday evening helped him take the first tee on the second day in just the right mood to let Turnberry have its own back. His performance was a knock out. His 63 was just one stroke away from being the most historic round in any major championship.

Greg is one of the elite few on the international scene who is capable of producing electrifying scoring bursts. On every circuit – in Japan, Australia, Europe and America – there are dozens of golfers grinding out a living with hard-worked-for scores of one, two or three under par. Greg goes for far more dramatic sub-par numbers. It is an ambition of his to shoot a 59 one day somewhere and I am not prepared to bet against his achieving it. When he was playing in the European Open at magnificent Sunningdale a few years ago, he announced that because the course was playing shorter than normal, he hoped to break 60 on it. Many scoffed and chortled at his apparent big-headedness. In fact he was not joking. He meant what he said. He did not achieve it that time but he tried really hard to match his words.

What is it that distinguishes the really low scorer from his rivals in the world of professional golf? Well, initially no golfer is going to rip a course apart if he has not got supreme confidence in his game, a fiercely positive approach, built-in power and, above all, no fear. Greg Norman admits the game does not scare him. His motto might well be "Live by the sword, die by the sword." He goes for the flag almost every time.

He explains his attitude this way: "I only look at the pin. I know the yardage I've got to hit and know that I can usually hit within six feet of the hole with pitching clubs. There may be a cluster of bunkers guarding the entrance to the green on the left and a water hazard along the right side of the green, but they do not figure in my thinking. If I let them interfere I'd start getting scared, apprehensive, defensive. So I block them out. Other people might find it difficult to do that. I'm lucky I don't."

Basically Norman does not have much fear

in anything he does. He has flown and enjoyed co-piloting an F-16 American Air Force jet; he enjoys travelling fast in his Ferrari or Rolls Royce Cornicha or XJS-6, even if wife Laura does not particularly like him to, but he is always quick to point out he never pushes himself beyond what he believes are his capabilities. It has been the same for him on the golf course, right from the day as a young amateur at Royal Queensland he shot a thirteen-under-par 60. That was not in a competition but it gave an indication of what young Norman might achieve later in his pro career.

He was a late starter in the game. He did not get his first full set of clubs until he was nearly sixteen. That was in 1970 and he remembers the clubs cost his parents one hundred and fifty Australian dollars. At that time he played off twenty-seven. Within nine months, he had won his first golf event playing with his dad, and in less than two years, he was down to scratch and very quickly picking up the Queensland Junior Championship. Even then he was a big hitter. His early coaches encouraged him to hit full out, believing it was easier to build in control and accuracy later, than to perfect a controlled game first, then try to add in the power. They were right. Now his average drive on tour is over two hundred and seventy-four yards and he always has something in reserve. This helps considerably when it comes to overpowering the par-five holes... and his low rounds usually include one or more eagles.

"My caddie, Pete Bender, always says that the key to a low scoring round is playing the par-fives well," says Greg, who recalls one time at the famous Wentworth course near London eagling three of the par-five holes and being mad at not eagling the other after hitting the green in two shots. "That annoyed me," he said.

Norman, like Fuzzy Zoeller when he gets it going (he once made eight birdies in a row in 1976) or like Europe's Jose-Maria Canizares, who ended the second round of the Swiss Open in 1978 with five birdies in a row and started the third with six birdies and then an eagle, is not short on adrenalin when required. In 1977, for instance, when he first arrived in Europe, he turned up at Blairgowrie in picturesque Perthshire to play the stylish Martini tournament (sadly no longer on the calendar). It looked as if Howard Clark, the Ryder Cup golfer, was going to win until Norman, in driv-

ing rain, birdied five holes out of six from the turn, stormed home in 32 for a course record 66, and picked up the first prize cheque.

In Australia in 1978 he shot a closing round of 61 in the Lakes Open to come from six strokes behind and win by three. Ian Stanley was his victim that day. He has shot a 62 at Las Vegas and in the Canadian Open at Jack Nicklaus' tough Glen Abbey course and he has had a 62 on what could be described as his home course these days – Bay Hill, in Orlando, Florida. He lives on the complex developed by Arnold Palmer, with whom he often practices.

"I really did have a chance that day at Bay Hill to shoot 59," he recalls. "I was nine under par after fourteen and lipped out for birdies at the last four holes." That he remembers, but most of his low scoring performances he has long forgotten. "Basically I'm not a record hunter," he says.

Power off the tee he most certainly has – the result, perhaps, of the fact that like Seve Ballesteros and Gary Player he has arms one inch longer than normal. He can build up a longer, wider arc and generate more power. He has broad shoulders and strong thigh muscles to help drive his legs through the shot. Although for over a year he was hampered by having caught an at-first untraceable virus in Hong Kong, Norman is incredibly fit and strong, even if he will not be able, according to his great friend Jack Nicklaus, to keep hitting the ball with such venom for much longer. Norman's longest drive by the way was one of 484 yards at the eighteenth at Gleneagles in Scotland. It was downhill and downwind, but still a monster shot. He finished just a yard or so from the green and eagled the hole to win his match in one of the BBC pro-celebrity encounters. (The following day Tom Watson, not to be outdone, hit his drive at the same hole a couple of yards further).

Norman's short game these days is sharper than it has ever been. He putts boldly, sometimes too boldly for the hole, but is good on the greens. Yet all that plus an ability to hit crisp irons into the green is not enough to make a golfer a regular low scorer. He needs that aggressive attitude and you might think that Greg inherited that from his parents. In fact, in the early days, Norman's off-course personality was painfully quiet. "I used to be very shy. I never used to talk. When I won my first pro event, (only the fourth tournament he had ever played in) I was drawn the following week with Nicklaus, my life-long hero. My whole game was modelled on his technique learned from poring over *Golf My Way* but I was dreadfully nervous. We met and chatted briefly the day before. He did most of the talking. When it came time to tee up, I topped my opening drive thirty yards and finished up shooting an 80. In those days I used to answer Press questions with a "yes" or "no", but I realised this was silly. I appreciated very quickly that if you can relate to people, and them to you, then that is the whole deal right there. Now I speak my mind and if I'm irritated by a question in the press room I am inclined to let the man who asked it have it if he deserves it." Greg has certainly conquered his shyness!

What he has not quite mastered yet is the necessity at times to throttle back, pull in the reins. If he is in the mood for a low score – and that is something that just seems to happen on the day – his natural approach is to go for it all the time, when some times a little conservatism might be a more prudent policy. Yet spectators love it when he is chasing the birdies and eagles with relentless enthusiasm, like he did on the second day at Turnberry. His 63 included an eagle and eight birdies. He dropped three shots, made only six pars, and thrilled the huge crowd that followed him as he proved that Turnberry could be mastered.

"I felt good when I got up that morning. The weather was better. On the way to the first tee I kept saying over and over in my mind 'Blue skies and a 65.' I say that often to myself to get myself going – and I moved into top gear quickly. I birdied three of the first four holes. Everything seemed to flow," recalled Norman afterwards. "The ball was coming off the middle of the club and I felt really confident and comfortable with my swing. I liked the speed of the greens. That suited me, too. There were no distractions. I was totally involved in each shot and that is when I am at my most dangerous. That day everything seemed just right."

The crowd were quickly behind him. Any gallery loves a golfer making birdies with the ease others are making pars. Norman, on the second day at Turnberry, reminded some of us of Johnny Miller in 1974 when in back-to-back weeks in the Arizona desert he shot twenty-four under par and twenty-five under par respectively at Phoenix and Tucson. Miller played, then, as if in a trance and Norman, blessed with the same low scoring ability to shoot lights out when "in the mood," was in spectacular form as he chased his first major title. The driver is his favourite club in the bag, but many golfers, fearful of ending up in the punishing rough, were using irons off the tee or three woods. Norman, crashing his way round, used his driver nine times and single-putted nine times for a score that matched the Open Championship record, the record for any major championship and the course record for Turnberry. Yet despite the fact that only Severiano Ballesteros later in the week would come close to matching Norman's performance in much easier conditions with a 64, the big Australian ended up being just a little disappointed. Over aggression had cost him an eagle at the seventeenth and he had to make do with a birdie. At the last he needed a birdie for 61, par for 62 but what he did not know was that that 62 would have been the lowest round ever in a major. Had he known so, he might not have been so aggressive with his first putt, which went sliding three feet past. Incredibly he missed the return and the record he now admits he would have loved most of all. "I reckon a 62 will never be broken in one of the majors and I just hope I get another chance to shoot it some where along the line," he said, turning his disappointment into positive thoughts for the future.

You know Greg Norman might just get another chance at that 62 and not miss out next time. He might just fire that 59 somewhere around the world because he is one of the elite few who are not scared of stringing birdies together and shooting low numbers. He loves it…and so do we all. His 63 on the second day of the Open paced the way for his eventual victory…and scores like that again in the future will ensure he lands more major titles while giving maximum pleasure to those watching him. Norman justifiably earns big money on the course and four times as much off it. His brand of aggressive golf is great for the game. Birdies and eagles draw in the crowds – and Norman is the latest in the line of international stars with a remarkable gift. He reminded us of that at Turnberry that Open Championship Friday.

THIRD ROUND RESULTS

Hole	1	2	3	4	5	6	7	8	9	10	11	12	13	14	15	16	17	18		
Par	4	4	4	3	4	3	5	4	4	4	3	4	4	4	3	4	5	4	Total	
Greg Norman	3	4	4	3	3	5	4	3	5	5	3	5	4	5	3	5	5	5	– 74	– 211
Tsuneyuki Nakajima	4	4	4	3	4	3	4	5	3	4	3	4	4	5	3	6	4	4	– 71	– 212
Ian Woosnam	4	4	4	3	5	2	4	4	4	3	3	4	6	5	2	4	5	4	– 75	– 214
Gordon J. Brand	4	4	4	3	5	4	4	4	5	5	4	4	4	3	4	5	5	5	– 72	– 214
Gary Koch	5	4	5	3	4	3	4	4	4	2	4	5	5	3	5	5	3		– 72	– 217
Jose-Maria Canizares	4	4	3	3	4	2	5	4	4	5	3	4	6	6	3	4	5	4	– 73	– 217
Nick Faldo	5	4	5	3	4	3	5	5	4	4	3	4	4	5	4	5	5	4	– 76	– 217
David Graham	4	4	4	2	3	3	5	4	5	4	3	4	5	4	3	4	5	4	– 70	– 218
Sam Torrance	4	5	5	3	5	3	4	5	4	4	2	3	3	5	3	4	5	4	– 71	– 218
Raymond Floyd	4	5	5	2	4	3	5	4	4	4	3	5	4	3	3	5	5	5	– 73	– 218
Bernhard Langer	5	4	4	3	4	4	5	5	4	4	3	4	5	4	3	6	5	4	– 76	– 218

HOLE SUMMARY

Hole	Par	Eagles	Birdies	Pars	Bogeys	Higher	Rank	Average
1	4	0	5	49	22	1	10	4.25
2	4	0	11	50	14	2	14	4.09
3	4	0	3	27	41	6	2	4.65
4	3	0	12	63	2	0	17	2.87
5	4	0	11	43	21	2	11	4.18
6	3	0	5	45	22	5	6	3.35
7	5	4	29	38	6	0	18	4.60
8	4	0	5	40	30	2	8	4.39
9	4	0	5	42	28	2	9	4.35
Out	35	4	86	397	186	20		36.73
10	4	0	13	48	13	3	15	4.08
11	3	0	9	52	16	0	13	3.09
12	4	0	2	29	37	9	1	4.73
13	4	0	2	43	28	4	7	4.44
14	4	0	1	37	36	3	3	4.53
15	3	0	10	49	18	0	12	3.10
16	4	0	5	37	24	11	3	4.53
17	5	0	13	51	8	5	16	5.06
18	4	0	1	43	28	5	5	4.51
In	35	0	56	389	208	40		38.07
Total	70	4	142	786	394	60		74.80

LOW SCORES

Low First Nine	Manuel Pinero	32
Low Second Nine	Philip Parkin	33
	Sam Torrance	33
Low Round	Ho Ming Chung	69

Players Below Par	1
Players At Par	5
Players Above Par	71

THE THIRD DAY
A Test Of Everyone's Patience

By Michael Williams

In the early afternoon of the third day a nuclear submarine nosed quietly along the shore line of Turnberry Bay. Someone playfully remarked that it had come to spirit away the Americans while no one was looking. But no rubber dinghies were seen paddling out and soon the submarine changed its bearing, heading southwest by west towards Ailsa Craig. Then it dived into the grey depths of the Firth of Clyde. It was the best place for it. A brisk southerly wind was springing up, the sky darkening and with it a strong suggestion of rain to follow that which had fallen for a time before lunch. All morning the traffic had been lined up nose-to-tail from Ayr to the north and Girvan to the south, but the crowds had come well prepared, wise to a British summer. Anoraks, waterproofs and umbrellas were going to be as essential to watching as patience was going to be to the golfers.

The scoreboard told its own story. All day only one player beat 70 and that was Ho Ming Chung, of Taiwan, who had a 69. As he was out at ten minutes to nine, he was done and finished long before the leaders had even started, fortunate to have had what reasonable weather there was going. Reasonable was a word he would hardly have chosen. Ho found it "very cold and miserable out there," particularly towards the end when he dropped shots at the sixteenth and eighteenth to see a potential 67 disappear. That too was to set a

pattern.

Whereas on Thursday in the first round the wind had helped down the closing holes, now it hindered. The seventeenth, which had averaged 4.36 on the first day and 4.35 on the second, shot up to 5.06. And there were no eagles as compared to the ten in the previous two rounds. Conversely the seventh, which is played in the opposite direction, dropped to an average of 4.60. Scores had to be made going out, salvaged coming home.

For all that, this third round was to prove marginally the easier day, as compared to Thursday, though not of course Friday. Four players this time matched par, Ian Woosnam again being one of them, which indicated his competitiveness when pitting himself against the elements. Others came from Sandy Lyle, the defending champion, Danny Edwards of America, Manuel Pinero from Spain, and David Graham, the widely experienced Australian.

Others of course fared less well, the most notable victim being Greg Norman, whose two-stroke lead at the end of the second round twice advanced to five on the way to the turn but, at the end of the day, had dwindled to only one. When within sight of making his first major championship a foregone conclusion, the big Australian had taken 40 to come home.

Tsuneyuki (Tommy) Nakajima, followed by an army of Japanese photographers, was on the other hand home in a highly adventurous 37 for a 71 and thereby lodged himself right on the heels of the leader. Moreover the championship was now wide open. Woosnam's 70 meant that he was now equal third instead of sixth and only three strokes behind, alongside Gordon J. Brand, who had lost a stroke on Norman with a 75.

Also still in touch were Nick Faldo (76), Jose-Maria Canizares (73) and the American Gary Koch (72), all sharing fifth place six strokes adrift, but less room for manoeuver from Graham, Sam Torrance (71), Raymond Floyd (73) and Bernhard Langer (76). With seven strokes to make up, something clearly exceptional was going to be needed as well as a further collapse from Norman.

Among those who were definitely out of it were Jack Nicklaus, whose 76 left him hopelessly placed at now seventeen over par and sixteen strokes behind Norman, Tom Watson (77 for 225), Seve Ballesteros (73 for 224) and Lyle (70 for 221), though the latter had very nearly got himself back into contention in defence of his title.

Lyle's opening rounds of 78 and 73 were hardly propitious, but when he went out in 34 and then continued steadily down the difficult homeward stretch, he began to have visions of a 68 or even perhaps a 67 which would, he felt, have given him the chance of getting up into the top four or five, if not quite winning.

He was certainly one of the few players strong enough to get close enough to the seventeenth green for the birdie he knew he needed, but it was this hole that finished him. His drive did not quite hold up in the wind and it pitched on the steep bank to the left of the fairway. Moreover, it found a ghastly lie in the now wet and clinging grass, against the grain. Not even his great strength could move the ball more than two feet.

Lyle's next went further, but it scooted across the fairway into more thick rough and he could only get another wedge to that recovery. His fifth shot had to be played with as much as a six iron and even that missed the green, going into the rough once again. From there he managed to get down in two, but his seven was altogether too much to bear.

Perhaps the most significant aspect of Norman's round was not so much that he twice failed to build on a lead of five strokes but that he kept smiling even when he could not "stop the bleeding," which is one of the ways

the professionals have of describing a succession of bogeys. It revealed an inner confidence in himself and a belief that in the end all would be well.

For a time it had looked even better than that. Norman began boldly with a perfect one iron to split the opening fairway, a five iron to ten feet and a putt which just caught the edge of the hole before dropping. Better was to follow. Only one of his pars through the next three holes needed the help of a single putt and then came a second birdie with an outrageous putt from the very edge of the green at the fifth. Two under par, five ahead of the field, the Australian was once again on the march.

At once he tripped. Downwind, the sixth was playing only a five iron against a one iron on the first day. But Norman may have struck the shot a shade too easily, came off it and in it went into the deep bunker on the right. From there he came out very short, which was excusable from beneath the deep face, and then putted short, which was not. His putt for a four missed and one wondered if the pressure was not getting to him again.

Norman rode this double bogey implacably. A three wood and five iron was enough to get him home in two at the 528-yards seventh for a birdie and then came another at the next where an immense drive left him with only a wedge to the green. His putt for a three was nevertheless substantial. Five ahead once again.

It was then that the tide, in golfing terms, began to turn. In his next ten holes, Norman had six bogeys and five pars. He was hanging on, but only just. At the ninth he was in the left rough from the tee and he could not get home in two. At the tenth he was through the green. At the twelfth he needed two drivers and was in the rough again. At the fourteenth his four iron second found more rough. At the sixteenth he drove into a bunker and had no chance of getting across the burn. And finally, at the eighteenth, not even two driver shots were long enough to reach the green in now drenching rain. Every one of them ugly fives.

"The difficulty of the rain was that you could not see," said Norman later, his hair still plastered flat by the downpour. "It was coming down horizontally and every time I looked up to see where I was going, it hit you in the face and stung. At the ninth and tenth I pulled the trigger too soon. Getting prepared to hit was the difficulty."

A caddie at such times is essential. Even so

Norman's hands slipped on the club twice, once at the twelfth and again at the fourteenth. His thoughts were centred on simply getting back in and not hurting himself with a triple or even quadruple bogey. The whole of this inward half had been played in rain and as Norman came up the last fairway he was hardly conscious of this even being the Open Championship. "Nearly everyone had gone," he said. No one could blame them.

Bearing in mind the glasses he has to wear, Nakajima's 71 was the bravest of efforts, particularly under the pressure he must have felt as a Japanese golfer, though not the first, within sight of a major championship. He did it moreover despite a six at the sixteenth. Here he found the fairway with his drive, but now it needed not a pitch to the green but a two iron to clear the burn. Even that was not enough. His ball rolled back down the bank from where he had to pick out under penalty and then took three more to hole out.

It was for all that a scrambling round, particularly coming home when the Japanese had no less than five single putts. Two holes stood out as an example of his ability to get something out of nothing. There may have been no more wild shot all week than Nakajima's four iron at the twelfth, careering right and coming to rest in thick rough on the wrong side of the hill that is topped by a war memorial.

He had no sight of the green at all but, with one huge heave, Nakajima somehow propelled the ball up and over the mound and on to the green. It was the most audacious of strokes and then he capped it all by holing a putt of a good five yards for his par four.

Later, having been in trouble off the tee at the seventeenth, Nakajima needed as much as a three wood for his third but struck it as clean as a whistle through the wind and rain to twenty-five feet and again holed the putt, this time for a birdie. Marvellous stuff indeed, further capped with another retrieve at the last where his pitch from the rough was beautifully judged to catch the mound and bring his ball back to within five feet of the hole.

Other pars had been saved at the tenth and thirteenth and for someone who admitted to feeling very excited, no one surely conquered their nerves better. As a child, Nakajima had seen pictures of the Open. Now he was right in the thick of it, with the whole of Japan, he knew, urging him on.

Woosnam, of stocky build, is well equipped for bad weather. What helped, he said, was that the two-ball play at least kept everybody moving at a good pace and he was able therefore to keep warm. His only wait was on the eighteenth and furthermore, he got through the last four holes in one under par.

His birdie had come at the fifteenth where a one iron came to rest only two feet from the flag. There was a pitch and single putt to save par at the sixteenth, but on the seventeenth and eighteenth the little Welshman played perfectly with two putts in each case. No one else played with such resolution over this stretch when the elements were at their most demanding.

The one hole that really hurt Woosnam was the thirteenth. Another foot to the left and he would have missed the bunker off the tee. As it was he was in the sand, came out but then hit a five iron over the back of the green and took three more to get down for a six. There then followed a five at the fourteenth and those three dropped strokes undid the birdies he had had at the sixth, seventh and tenth.

Even so Woosnam was delighted with his position and it bothered him not at all if the wind were to continue to blow on the last day. European golfers are as a whole more used to it than Americans, he remarked.

Gordon J. Brand suffered most of his damage around the middle of the course. He took three putts for a five at the fifth and, like Norman, his partner, was in the bunker short and right at the sixth. This cost him a four against the Australian's five.

Despite finding another bunker at the seventh, Brand still managed a birdie, but he could not find the green at either the ninth or tenth, which proved costly. When he did hit the green at the short eleventh, he then three-putted. This was a bad run but the unassuming Yorkshireman rallied with a whole string of pars through to the eighteenth, thanks to some solid holing out and yielded only at the last after pushing his drive.

Of the Americans, Koch got himself into the most challenging position with a 72 for a share of fifth place. He has become a great supporter of the Open and loves the challenge of a British links, quite undeterred by the vagaries of the weather.

Golf, he believes, has become too automatic in the States where everything is done by yardages, or tends to be. In Britain clubbing takes on a whole new dimension according to the wind and, like Nicklaus and Watson before him, he enjoys having to use his brain rather than referring to map references.

Another American who might just have got himself into the picture was D.A. Weibring. His 76 included an eight at the eighteenth. Here he pulled a two-iron second into the rough and got such a bad lie that his attempted recovery with a sand wedge succeeded only in driving the ball even deeper into the long grass. Another attempt advanced him, he swore, no more than an inch and then he shanked. How easily they can all add up. Furthermore, the same hole had cost him a six in the second round.

If this put Weibring out of the championship, Raymond Floyd admitted that his chances of winning the two Opens in the same year were gone too. The U.S. champion had a 73 and no luck at all. He twice missed short putts while four others looked in all the way, but still stayed out. He felt that he had played well but got absolutely nothing out of it.

Briefly, little Manuel Pinero looked as if he could get into the thick of the fight, particularly when he went through the turn in 32. He had thoughts then of a 66, which would have meant one more birdie. It came at the seventeenth but what he had not bargained for were the bogeys he had at the twelfth and fourteenth and a double-bogey six at the sixteenth. He took three putts at the fourteenth when going for a birdie and another three at the sixteenth. But the damage here was more a four iron second short and left into the rough. He was in two minds over the shot and in the end fell between the two stools.

The high hopes that rested on Faldo and Langer tended to fade with their 76s and it was therefore Woosnam and the elder Brand who took the greatest expectation of another home victory into the last round. But everything, no one needed telling, was going to depend on Norman. Once again the promised land was beckoning.

Greg Norman posted 74 in the wind and rain of the third round. He led Tsuneyuki Nakajima by one stroke

Tsuneyuki Nakajima fought the elements but returned a 71 despite hitting into the burn at the sixteenth (bottom left)

Gary Koch (left) led the American challenge and D. A. Weibring (right) also played well

David Graham (218) and Payne Stewart (220)

Nick Faldo (above) soared to 76, while Ian Woosnam (right) returned a 70 for joint third

Peter Alliss and Tony Jacklin observed from the tower as BBC cameramen and other still photographers covered the course

COMMENTARY
The End Of America's Dominance
By Alister Nicol

There is a general acceptance that the modern Open Championship did not begin until 1960. The oldest championship in golf did not, to be sure, ever sink out of sight and, for those with ambition, it was very much a prize to be sought after. However, after the legendary Ben Hogan travelled to triumph at Carnoustie in 1953, the lustre of the championship dulled somewhat, particularly for those professionals pursuing their careers in the United States.

Indeed, after Sam Snead won the first post-war championship at St. Andrews in 1946, there was only one other winner under the Stars and Stripes banner until 1961, and that was Hogan. In 1953 the tough little Texan had already come first in the U.S. Masters and U.S. Open before heading for the coast of Angus to make his deliberate and meticulous preparations for the Open Championship, preparations that were to prove irresistibly sound. So superior was Hogan that year that there are many who will insist that the impregnable quadrilateral – the Grand Slam – would have been his had he been able to take advantage of the jet-age travel which so many globe-trotting circuit stars take so much for granted nowadays. Hogan could not even attempt the Grand Slam because the return journey from Carnoustie took so long he was unable to make it to Birmingham, Michigan, in time to challenge winner Walter Burkemo, or anyone else for that matter, in the U.S. PGA Championship, which was then still a match-play event.

Outside of Hogan the Open in the Fifties was very much a British Empire affair. Peter Thomson won four times, Arthur D'Arcy (Bobby) Locke three times, with Max Faulkner (1951) and young Gary Player (1959) also getting into the act.

Then came 1960. In that year a thirty-two-year-old out of Latrobe, Pennsylvania, burst onto the American golfing scene in a big, big way. Arnold Palmer emulated Hogan in winning both the U.S. Masters and the U.S. Open before deciding to fulfill a life-long ambition and enter the Open. As a youngster he had longed to visit the home of golf and play the links courses he had read and heard so much about but finance, or rather the lack of it, had precluded such an adventure. But in 1960 he came, he saw – and he almost conquered. Despite a storming final round of 68 he lost out by the narrowest of margins to Australia's Kel Nagle.

That first Palmer Open, however, was to have a profound effect on future championships. On the way home from a rain-lashed St. Andrews, Arnold vowed that he would return to Britain to win the oldest title in the game and he did so the following year at Royal Birkdale then repeated in 1962 at Troon. While his performances on the golf course were significant, it was Palmer's conduct off the course that was most telling. He never lost

73

an opportunity, as his career took off in America hand in hand with the boom in purses and television interest, to persuade fellow American players that until they played and won in Britain they could not regard themselves as true champions or great golfers. In effect he became the greatest ambassador for the Open the Royal and Ancient Golf Club could ever have hoped to recruit. His influence was immeasurable.

The facts speak for themselves. Since Palmer's first victory in 1961 there have been twenty-six Opens, seventeen of them won by Americans. Indeed, between 1961 only Bob Charles (1963), Roberto de Vicenzo (1967), Gary Player (1968 and 1974), and Tony Jacklin (1969) were able to stem the American tide until Severiano Ballesteros won at Royal Lytham in 1979. American dominance was almost total. For a long, long time the rest of the golfing world firmly believed that the U.S. tour was the strongest in the world, that American players were virtually unbeatable. The rest of the world, so to speak, were in the minor league, at least one step removed from the very best who had the benefit of playing, we were lead to believe, on the finest courses, in the finest conditions and with the added bonus of excellent practice facilities on which to sharpen and fine-tune their swings.

Turnberry, 1986, proved that is no longer the case. There were only five American players in the leading twenty. Gary Koch was joint sixth, eight strokes behind Greg Norman, to be the highest-ranking American. The order of finish was instead filled by European, Australian and Japanese stars, not only major champions Bernhard Langer, Severiano Ballesteros and David Graham, but also such players as Gordon J. Brand, the runner-up to Norman by five strokes; Ian Woosnam, Nick Faldo, Brian Marchbank, Christy O'Connor, Jr., Jose-Maria Canizares, Tsuneyuki Nakajima, Anders Forsbrand and Jose-Maria Olazabal.

The third day of the championship this year was memorable for the comments of two of the most respected and influential voices in the world of golf over the last couple of decades. Jack Nicklaus, who languished sixteen strokes adrift of Norman with one round to play (and finished eighteen behind), refused to join in the criticism of the tough way the course had been set up. Said Nicklaus, "Most of the criticism seems to be coming from players with high scores. These are the guys you hear com-

plain and maybe they should keep their mouths shut." Somewhat more outspoken was Mark McCormack. He accused several players of being "cry-babies" and suggested that certain American players were "pampered."

Whether or not they were pampered cry-babies is not for me to say. What is abundantly clear in the aftermath of Turnberry, 1986, is that American golf no longer sits impregnably at the top of the heap. And I do not think it is because American standards have fallen off. I am certain it is because non-American golfers have become better and better. They are no longer in awe of American golf. Reasons for this are not too hard to detect either. Around a decade or so ago European golfers, in particular, packed their clubs, collected a bundle of air tickets and escaped the harsh winters of Northern Europe by fleeing to any warmer clime where golf was played. They ventured to Africa, Australia, the Far East, South Africa. In doing so they were learning all the time. Learning how to cope with time zones, different foods, indifferent courses, enthusiastic but often bumbling officialdom. In short, they became better all-round players.

Even in the comparatively narrow confines of the European Tour a multitude of variations had to be faced and overcome. Some weeks, say in Spain, they would play American-type courses with fast and true putting surfaces, the next on some inland course in Britain where a cold winter followed by a poor spring meant putting on greens that resembled corrugated iron. Some grumbled, groused and groaned. But on the whole they buckled down and bit the bullet. Some threw in their lot with the "major" league to further improve their technique. Ballesteros, Langer and Faldo, to name but three, crossed the Atlantic, taking with them the skills learned round the globe and proved they could win in golf's Valhalla as well as in some golfing versions of Hades.

Perhaps the big turn-around came at Augusta in 1980 when the supremely-talented Ballesteros, harshly called the "Car Park Champion" following his Open success some months previously at Royal Lytham, became the first Spaniard to don the green jacket. When he won the U.S. Masters again in 1983 it was an enormous fillip to Tony Jacklin's Ryder Cup side, who came within a point of beating America on captain Jack Nicklaus' home territory in September of that year. Indeed there is a school of thought that had Bernard Gallacher not been running a temperature of more than one hundred degrees that humid final afternoon in the last singles against Tom Watson, Europe's long-awaited first win on American soil would have been achieved three years ago.

The signs were there then – the second division players were on the march, hungry for promotion.

In 1984 Ballesteros danced an unforgettable fandango of joy on the eighteenth green of the Old Course after holing a putt for the birdie-three he knew had earned him his second Open, having seen Tom Watson's bid for a record-equalling sixth come to grief on the road at seventeen following an over-bold approach. The Pretenders were growing in strength almost by the hour it seemed. Came the U.S. Masters in 1985, and Bernhard Langer was the first German to win. On to Royal St. George's for the Open, and Scotland's Sandy Lyle emerged as the winner. He and Langer joined Ballesteros to help Tony Jacklin's European team win the Ryder Cup. The American team had no Nicklaus or Watson but, as Lee Trevino said before the historic match at The Belfry, what he did have was a team comprised of the best twelve golfers on the tour at that time qualified to play for Uncle Sam.

When the golfing circus came to Turnberry in 1986 they found the most perfectly-manicured course in recent Open history, probably the best-ever in fact. The rough, however, was ferocious and far too many players, it seemed to me, were at least three down as they stood on the first tee. It was certainly un-American. But, going back to 1960 and the advent of Palmer, it was that very un-Americanism that was the charm, the appeal of the Open. Over the years the Nicklauses, Watsons and Crenshaws, have not wanted watered fairways and soft, holding greens. They have looked forward eagerly to testing their skills on natural linksland, keenly anticipating the fullest examination of their abilities to overcome new challenges.

By the same token, however, Turnberry 1986 was something else for non-American players as well. The yelps of anguish from Ballesteros and many others proved that the Royal and Ancient Championship Committee had not by any means come up with a course which favoured those not reared on American-style golf. And Tsuneyuki (Tommy) Nakajima, fancied by many to win until he three-putted the fifty-fifth hole from nowhere, could not find words to express his feelings after his first practice round. Not even in Japanese!

Oriental golf is nothing new, despite Nakajima's run at Norman for three rounds at Turnberry. Back in 1971 at Royal Birkdale an ever-smiling Lu Liang Huan (Mr. Lu to the world) hunted Lee Trevino right to the line, and in 1985 only a drastic double-hit robbed Chen Tze Chung of the honour of becoming the first Taiwanese winner of the U.S. Open. For a long time Jumbo Ozaki and Isao Aoki led the charge of the Japanese onto the links. There can be little question that Nakajima is now the main man from the land of cars, raw fish and saki. In Japan alone Nakajima has won more than two million pounds sterling and is a genuine superstar. Had he held on to oust Norman he would, in all probability, have been awarded his country's Master of Sport honour. That is an award made only twice before, to a baseball player and a judo expert.

Nakajima's previous best finish in the Open was seventeenth at St. Andrews in 1978 when, having forced himself into contention, he hit the Road Hole in two super shots in the often-fateful third round. He then putted into the Road bunker and proceeded to flail away like a dervish. A birdie-three had seemed possible, but poor Tommy eventually signed for a nine. That, though, was not his highest score of the season, for in the U.S. Masters his inscrutability was tested to the full when he took thirteen at the thirteenth. Nevertheless, Far Eastern golf is coming ever closer to uncovering a player capable of winning a major title and giving American golf even more problems. A total of fifteen million golfers in Japan, eighteen thousand courses and more than six thousand driving ranges would appear to be ideal conditions for breeding an Open champion. Golfers round the globe are truly crowding onto the platform which has launched three non-American Open champions in three years.

I will not accept any arguments that Norman won only because he has been playing in the States these last few years. Like Ballesteros, Langer, Nakajima and a host of others, the 1986 champion has been a member of the "Have Clubs, Will Travel" brigade.

Maybe Mark McCormack was right, maybe the current U.S. crop is pampered. Maybe they will have to broaden their horizons if they are once more to dominate. Let's wait and see.

FOURTH ROUND RESULTS

Hole	1	2	3	4	5	6	7	8	9	10	11	12	13	14	15	16	17	18	Total	
Par	4	4	4	3	4	3	5	4	4	4	3	4	4	4	3	4	5	4		
Greg Norman	4	4	3	3	5	3	5	3	4	4	4	4	4	3	3	4	5	4	– 69	– 280
Gordon J. Brand	4	4	5	3	6	2	6	5	4	4	3	3	4	4	3	4	3	4	– 71	– 285
Bernhard Langer	4	4	5	3	4	3	4	5	4	3	3	3	3	5	3	4	4	4	– 68	– 286
Ian Woosnam	4	5	5	3	3	3	4	5	4	5	4	5	4	3	3	4	4	4	– 72	– 286
Nick Faldo	4	4	4	3	5	3	5	4	4	4	2	4	4	4	3	4	5	4	– 70	– 287
Seve Ballesteros	4	3	4	2	4	3	4	4	5	3	3	4	4	3	3	3	4	4	– 64	– 288
Gary Koch	4	4	4	3	4	4	4	4	4	4	3	5	4	4	3	4	5	4	– 71	– 288
Fuzzy Zoeller	4	4	4	2	4	4	4	5	4	4	3	4	4	4	3	5	4	3	– 69	– 289
Brian Marchbank	4	3	4	2	5	3	4	4	3	5	3	4	4	5	2	5	5	4	– 69	– 289
Tsuneyuki Nakajima	6	4	5	3	4	3	4	5	4	4	3	5	4	4	3	5	6	5	– 77	– 289

HOLE SUMMARY

Hole	Par	Eagles	Birdies	Pars	Bogeys	Higher	Rank	Average
1	4	0	7	57	11	1	13	4.08
2	4	0	12	46	17	1	12	4.09
3	4	0	5	46	23	2	9	4.29
4	3	0	15	52	8	1	16	2.93
5	4	0	4	44	22	6	5	4.42
6	3	0	5	41	27	3	2	3.37
7	5	1	28	35	12	0	17	4.76
8	4	0	1	32	35	8	1	4.66
9	4	0	5	34	33	4	3	4.47
Out	35	1	82	387	188	26		37.07
10	4	0	9	48	14	5	10	4.20
11	3	0	6	61	9	0	15	3.04
12	4	0	4	41	27	4	5	4.42
13	4	0	6	58	12	0	13	4.08
14	4	0	5	39	27	5	4	4.45
15	3	0	4	50	19	3	7	3.28
16	4	0	4	46	21	5	8	4.36
17	5	1	36	35	3	1	18	4.57
18	4	0	7	52	16	1	11	4.14
In	35	1	81	430	148	24		36.54
Total	70	2	163	817	336	50		73.61

LOW SCORES

Players Below Par	7		Low First Nine	Brian Marchbank	32
Players At Par	3		Low Second Nine	Seve Ballesteros	31
Players Above Par	66		Low Round	Seve Ballesteros	64

THE FOURTH DAY
A Major Victory, At Last

By Michael Williams

It was midnight. The crowds had long since gone with their own particular memories of another Open Championship. The sea breeze sighed gently through the gaunt grandstands, empty except for one small group of people. They had with them the championship trophy and a bottle of champagne, and among them was Greg Norman. Between sips, he reflected on the day's events. "It just seemed the thing to do," he reflected later. "It was a magic little interlude, savouring it all again, just with a few close friends." The police found them but let them be. They understood, not wanting to break the spell.

A whole galaxy of memories danced and interchanged in Norman's mind. He had done it at last and won a major championship; moreover it was the one he would always place before all others. As an Australian and a member of the Commonwealth, Norman has viewed the Open as always enjoying a special importance that may never be attained by the U.S. Open, Masters or PGA.

But for Norman it had been a long time coming. He was now thirty-one and there had begun to be doubts that he might never quite climb the game's highest mountains. Questions had not been asked about his game, which was invariably majestic, but about his nerve. Three times he had been close and three times he had failed. It was something of which he had been constantly reminded, though he

always took it with a smile and put it down to the learning process.

In the 1984 U.S. Open at Winged Foot he had scrambled like mad over the closing holes, culminating in the most outrageous four at the last where he sank a putt right across the green after hitting a long iron into a grandstand. It earned him a tie, but Fuzzy Zoeller was in a different class in the play-off.

Then, earlier this year at Augusta in the U.S. Masters, Norman had come to the eighteenth hole on the last day needing a birdie to beat Jack Nicklaus. No second shot could have been more reminiscent than that other second shot at Winged Foot. It cost the Australian even a tie as he took five. But opportunity was to beckon yet again in the U.S. Open at Shinnecock Hills a month before he came to Turnberry.

This time he led, at one point by three strokes in the third round and by a shot as he waited on the first tee for the last eighteen holes to begin. Already a spectator has accused him of "choking." Norman was not amused. Nor did he choke. He just faded quietly away, for some reason quite unable to get himself motivated.

All these things had played on Norman's mind, he reflected as he sat by the darkened eighteenth green at Turnberry, though now he had that inner warmth that comes with victory. He looked back twenty-four hours to when again, as in the U.S. Open, he nursed a slender one-stroke lead, this time from Tsuneyuki (Tommy) Nakajima. He remembered sitting in the dining room of the Turnberry Hotel that Saturday evening and he remembered Jack Nicklaus coming across and pulling up a chair.

No man in the whole golfing world is more familiar with the turmoil he knew must be going through the Australian's stomach, and head, too, for that matter. The essence of Nicklaus's brief conversation was that he believed Norman had everything that was now needed to win, that he would win and that he (Nicklaus) could think of no one he would rather win. "Just concentrate on the pressure of your grip," he advised. "That will orchestrate your tempo."

Norman was touched by the gesture, as he was, too, by other words of encouragement he received from such players as Fuzzy Zoeller, John Mahaffey and Hubert Green, who regretfully had to withdraw from the final round because of illness. That all these, who had been through this major championship mill themselves, seemed to really want him to win, was the spur.

The Australian spent a fitful night but did not rise from his bed until around 9.30 a.m. He felt nervous and that worried him. He had felt nervous, too, when only a few weeks before he had faced the last round of the U.S. Open. Slowly the morning passed until the appointed hour of 2.40 p.m. That knotted feeling in Norman's stomach still persisted but that was no bad thing. It is being able to control it that matters. The club still felt good in his hands, as good as it had felt all week. His state of mind was also positive. He felt determined that Turnberry should not get the better of him. He had a genuine desire not just to win but also to break par for the four rounds; to show that it could be done.

What was heartening also was that the weather had finally relented, as if to show what Turnberry could really be like. The sun had come out, the wind had dropped, and across the waters of the Firth of Clyde sprang Arran and the Mull of Kintyre in all their purple glory. This was a different, more manageable golf course and if Norman needed any proof, it came from the man who, at the beginning of the week, a good many people had expected to win. It was too late but Seve Ballesteros had finally come to life with a 64. From equal thirty-eighth place after sluggish rounds of 76, 75 and 73, Ballesteros shot up in the end to equal sixth and for the first time got a place on the leaderboard.

If Norman ever needed assurance that destiny was to be on his side, it was not long in coming. Indeed it could hardly have come sooner. His main challenger had to be Nakajima, with whom he was partnered. But to extend his one-stroke lead to three at the first hole was totally unpredictable, particularly after the Japanese had split the fairway with his opening tee shot.

There is more to the playing of a hole than that, however, and Nakajima then missed the green; not seriously but missing it nonetheless. All seemed well when he chipped to five or six feet but from there, quite incredulously, he took three putts for a six.

Norman could hardly believe his eyes, but dame fortune had not finished with him yet. At the third he bunkered his four-iron second and then holed the recovery from some twenty-five yards for a birdie. Such must have exceeded his wildest expectations as his lead increased even further. Yet even then the waters in which he sailed were not entirely smooth.

A drive into the left rough at the fifth and a six iron which left him there led to a five. The short sixth he got through without mishap, which was a relief, but then he hooked again from the tee high in the dunes at the seventh. Norman admitted to feeling "jumpy" and no one was quicker to see it than his caddie, Pete Bender. There, Bender noticed, was that dreaded quickening swing rearing its head again.

As Norman hacked his way back on to the fairway again, Bender drew alongside and said, "I want you to do everything at my pace. Just walk at my speed and we'll do fine." Those were words of sound advice. Norman saved his par and needed little further bidding. Out near the lighthouse he got a three at the eighth with a drive, four iron and short putt, and when he went through the ninth green beneath a grandstand, he lofted a lovely little pitch from the dropping area close enough to hole the putt. He was out in 34.

An eight iron into a bunker at the eleventh led to one more bogey but that stroke was retrieved with a seven-iron second to within a yard of the flag at the fourteenth. By now Norman knew that he could hardly lose. "Even I was impressed with some of my shots" he said later without a hint of boastfulness. Drives and irons rifled after one another and the only question was whether the Australian might establish a post-war-record winning margin.

This stood at six, by Arnold Palmer at Troon in 1962 and by Johnny Miller at Royal Birkdale in 1976. The chances were there, notably at the seventeenth where, after a drive into the right rough and a wedge back onto the fairway, he struck a six iron to five feet. By now, Norman's emotions were getting the better of him. He was playing by instinct as much as anything.

Norman could hardly see the hole, let alone read the putt, as he desperately tried to line it up. Not surprisingly perhaps, he missed it, having indeed to sink an even longer one coming back. At least he was able to enjoy his homecoming and, with a four at the last for an inward half of 35, he was round in 69. He had beaten par for the round but not for the championship. His total of 280 matched it and, all things considered, that may just about have been right.

The right man, and a very popular one, had triumphed and while his five-stroke winning margin from Gordon J. Brand was a convincing one, there had been just one moment when a gripping finish could have been in store. The threat had in fact not come from Brand, whose second place was due in the end to the eagle putt he holed for a three at the seventeenth, but from Bernhard Langer, who tied third with Ian Woosnam on 286, six strokes behind.

Very warm the West German's reception was, too, as he reached the last green, for only the night before he had learned that his wife, Vicki, had given birth to their first child, a daughter, Jackie Carol. Congratulations were emblazoned across the scoreboard at the beginning of the day and, as he putted out for his 68, there were cries of "Come on Dad," which he clearly appreciated.

And "come on" he certainly had when, after an outward half of 36 that had done nothing for his prospects, Langer suddenly began to fire a whole sheath of arrows at the flagsticks. Seven irons to the tenth and twelfth brought him birdie-threes, the latter coming to rest an inch from the hole, and then an eight iron to the thirteenth yielded the formality of a third birdie. So that was three threes in a row and there ought to have been a fourth at the fourteenth. Here his second shot actually hit the flagstick before glancing no more than six feet away.

Had it gone in for a two, which well it might

have done, the difference between him and Norman would have been only three strokes and that might have been very interesting. As it was, Langer failed not only to get a birdie but missed the one back as well. As with Ballesteros, the West German had reserved his best until last, which was too late. But, having now been second twice and third twice, his turn may well come.

Brand played above himself to finish runner-up. Nothing in his earlier-season form had suggested it any more than had his past record. Yet he kept his nerve, particularly in the last round when he could have vanished from sight. The Yorkshireman took 39 to reach the turn with three bogeys, one double bogey (at the fifth) and only one birdie, at the sixth. His driving was all awry and it was not until the twelfth that he found the fairway from the tee.

On reflection Brand thought that he might have been trying too hard. He worked out that perhaps he was not completing his backswing. But down the inward stretch he felt that he played "really well." A scrambled par at the tenth lifted his spirits and with a birdie at the twelfth they positively soared. From then on Brand was convinced that he could finish high. He did, home in 32, thanks in the end to that eagle at the seventeenth.

Woosnam, after a patchy outward half, was "killed" by a run of three bogeys from the tenth. It was one of those days when he could hole nothing on the greens. He had hoped that it might be windy and it was not. Birdies at the fourteenth and seventeenth hauled him back into a tie with Langer for third place, a stroke ahead of Nick Faldo, who was as consistent as anybody on this last day.

Faldo finished with a 70, his driving and long iron play delighting him. There was a bogey five at the fifth and a birdie at the eleventh. Otherwise all were pars. Such a high finish was, he felt, justification of all the hard work he had put into the re-construction of his swing.

Gary Koch, with a last round of 71, had meanwhile tied Ballesteros for sixth place on 288 and he was leading American. What a contrast to 1977 when eight Americans had filled the leading places. Such is the wheel of golfing fortune as, in a final salute to Norman and the first Australian victory since Peter Thomson in 1965, Concorde dipped its wings in a low-level fly-past.

FINAL LEADERS

Greg Norman	280
Gordon J. Brand	285
Bernhard Langer	286
Ian Woosnam	286
Nick Faldo	287
Seve Ballesteros	288
Gary Koch	288
Fuzzy Zoeller	289
Brian Marchbank	289
Tsuneyuki Nakajima	289

ATTENDANCE

Sunday	1,198
Monday	2,002
Tuesday	9,103
Wednesday	12,547
Thursday	25,545
Friday	28,787
Saturday	28,184
Sunday	25,596
	133,130

CHAMPIONSHIP HOLE SUMMARY

Hole	Par	Eagles	Birdies	Pars	Bogeys	Higher	Rank	Average
1	4	1	37	298	114	7	14	4.19
2	4	0	38	226	168	25	7	4.40
3	4	0	33	252	149	23	9	4.35
4	3	1	79	307	62	8	17	2.99
5	4	0	21	211	177	48	5	4.56
6	3	0	23	208	185	41	1	3.55
7	5	6	108	238	98	7	16	4.99
8	4	0	11	169	224	53	3	4.72
9	4	0	23	231	177	26	6	4.46
Out	35	8	373	2140	1354	238		38.21
10	4	0	44	240	135	38	8	4.38
11	3	0	65	308	80	3	15	3.05
12	4	0	13	213	187	43	4	4.59
13	4	0	29	297	112	18	11	4.26
14	4	0	12	174	210	60	2	4.73
15	3	0	46	295	110	5	13	3.16
16	4	0	50	258	100	48	10	4.34
17	5	17	228	180	24	7	18	4.51
18	4	0	31	298	110	17	12	4.25
In	35	17	518	2263	1068	239		37.27
Total	70	25	891	4403	2422	477		75.48

	First Round	Second Round	Third Round	Fourth Round	Total
Players Below Par	0	15	1	7	23
Players At Par	1	8	5	3	17
Players Above Par	151	128	71	66	416

THE CHAMPION'S CARD

Round	Hole	1	2	3	4	5	6	7	8	9	10	11	12	13	14	15	16	17	18	Total
	Par	4	4	4	3	4	3	5	4	4	4	3	4	4	4	3	4	5	4	— 70
One		4	3	4	2	6	3	5	4	4	4	4	6	4	5	3	5	4	4	— 74
Two		4	3	3	2	5	3	3	5	4	3	2	4	4	3	3	3	4	5	— 63
Three		3	4	4	3	3	5	4	3	5	5	3	5	4	5	3	5	5	5	— 74
Four		4	4	3	3	5	3	5	3	4	4	4	4	4	3	3	4	5	4	— 69

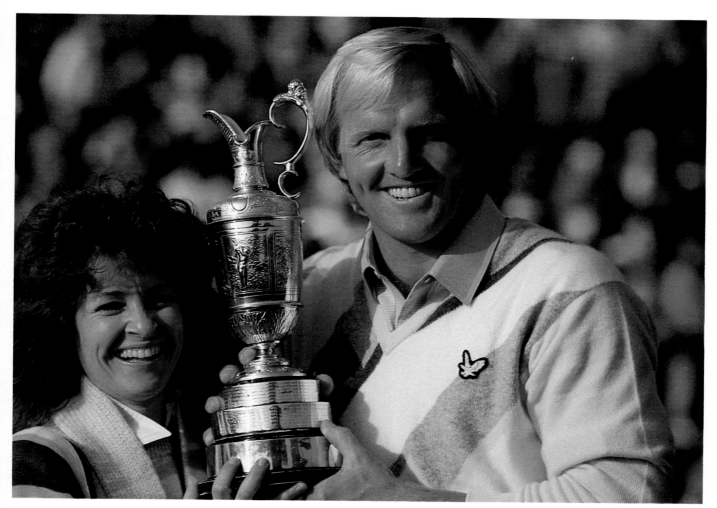

Laura and Greg Norman (above) pose with the Open Championship trophy. Tom Watson (right) was again denied a record-equalling sixth victory. Watson finished on 296, 16 strokes behind

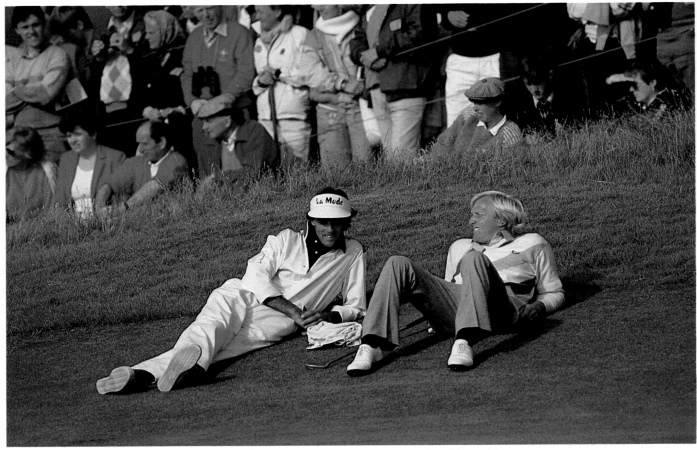

Accurate putting (next page) put Greg Norman and caddy Pete Bender in a comfortable position

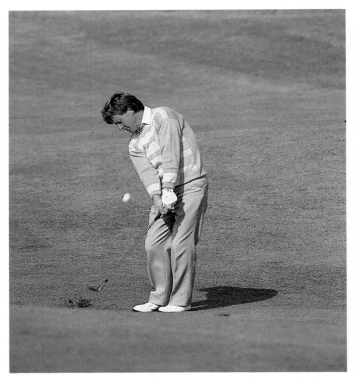

Ian Woosnam (left) placed joint third but Sam Torrance's chances were ruined by 78 in the first round and 76 in the last

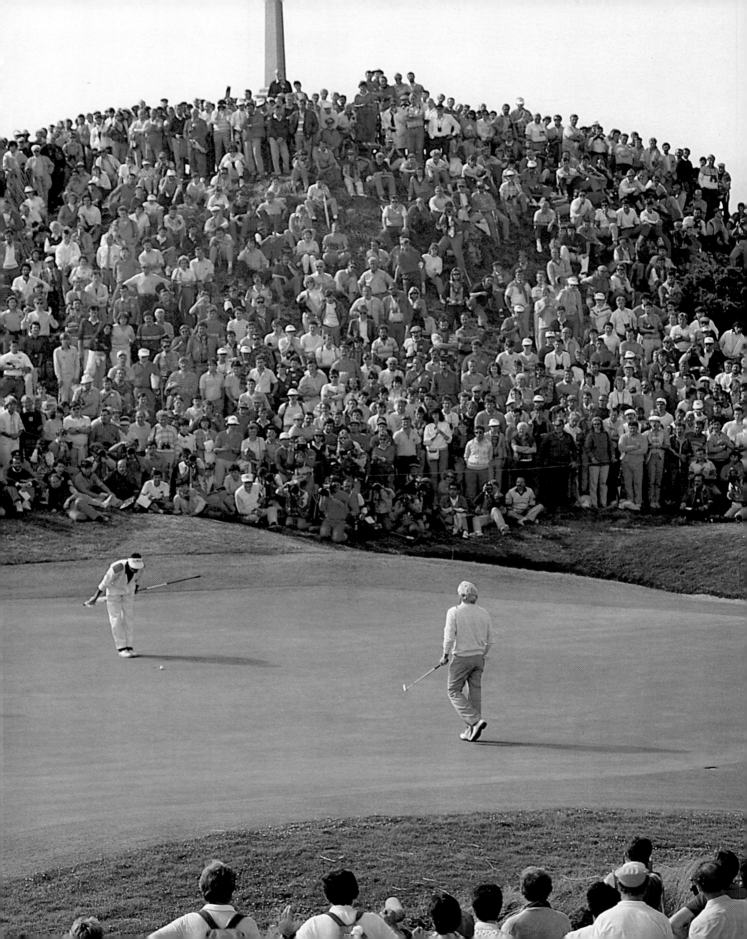

Gordon J. Brand (left) was runner-up and Brian Marchbank was the leading Scot

Bernhard Langer scored 76 in the third round, but that night his wife, Vikki, gave birth
to their first child. Langer finished with 68 for joint third with Ian Woosnam

Hours after Greg Norman emerged as Open champion, the Australian concluded his victory celebration with a try on the bagpipes

COMMENTARY
A Triumph Of Positive Attitude

By Norman Mair

The Norman Conquest, as it was all too predictably dubbed on all sides, was above all a triumph over course and conditions; a triumph which owed a great deal to a refreshing and determinedly positive attitude.

As Greg Norman pointedly noted, he was not exactly without experience of winds in his native Queensland, aside altogether from his years on the European Tour. Yet the cold and damp of much of Open Championship week was a further alien dimension for one reared in Australia and now living in Florida. That was one reason why, in the sanctuary of the last afternoon, one remembered the first morning when Norman was out in the worst of the weather. The four-over-par 74 he wrested from the hostile elements was at once a signal that he would not lightly accept that this was not to be his year and the highest opening round by an eventual winner since Gary Player at Carnoustie in 1968.

One recalled, too, the Saturday evening when, with almost all the field in, Norman found himself having to play the last three holes into the teeth of an icily stinging, windswept rain. He could have lost the Open then and there, but he laughed in the face of the storm. His eye fell on a lone and portly scribe, drenched to the skin despite his waterproofs. "You have to be mad to be out here," he called, good-humouredly. Despite his own increasingly unpropitious circumstances, Norman

also found amusement in the plight of Graham Simmers, the R&A official with the match. Taking duty to heroic lengths, Simmers weathered the storm simply in sodden blazer and flannels. (Some years ago, an American professional had refused to accept a ruling from no less a personage than John Salvesen, because Salvesen was not visibly clad in the familiar blazer and rosette).

It was painful and next-to-impossible to see ahead into the biting, horizontal rain and England's Gordon J. Brand was to exclaim afterwards, "How Greg and I hit the fairway at the seventeenth I'll never know."

Using a driver for his second, not least to hold it down in the wind, Norman found, disturbingly, that he had to alter his habitual pre-shot ritual wherein, initially, he has only his right hand on the club as he shapes to the shot. No matter how strenuously he and his caddie, the invaluable Pete Bender, towelled the grip, it was wet again by the time he placed his left hand on the club. Accordingly, he settled into his address with both hands on the club, resolutely refusing to allow the artificial change in routine to throw him.

At the conclusion of that penultimate round, Norman, wet, cold and with his lead shrivelled to but one stroke, came to the press tent. He asked ruefully if the interview could be kept relatively short. He spoke cheerfully, if graphically, of the ordeal of those finishing holes. A journalist more used to the tennis firmament marvelled anew. "These golfers," he muttered, "are a different breed."

None the less, for all his philosophical acceptance that the weather was integral to the storied lore of the Open, Norman was not slow to declare that he would much prefer to see the Open with two starting points, to give to all more nearly the same conditions. But, of course, apart from other considerations, only Birkdale and Muirfield of the Open Championship links in Britain lend themselves to such a suggestion, with the tenth tee suitably adjacent to the clubhouse.

A few years ago on the European Tour, an informal poll of some of the more celebrated caddies gave the vote for the longest, straightest driver unhesitatingly to Norman. Even so, Norman not only belonged vehemently among those who held that, especially for a wind-blown links, the fairways at Turnberry were too narrow but also he took colourful exception to the billowing, impenetrable rough.

Over in America, Norman observed, everyone sued everyone and there were mornings when there were more law suits in the air than golf balls. When, in Los Angeles, a burglar could tumble downstairs and successfully sue the occupant of the house he was rifling, might not a golfer who broke a wrist or tore a tendon endeavouring to get out of unreasonably high rough "have legal redress against the establishment?" *Volenti non fit injuria*, as they say in the caddie shed. In other words, no injustice is done to a person by an act to which he consents.

In fact, Craig Stadler was to damage tendons in his left wrist at the fourteenth in the first round so badly that he played no further part in the championship after an opening twelve-over-par 82. "I damned near broke my wrist in the rough," the Walrus bristled, "and I doubt if I moved the ball an inch!"

However, as Michael Bonallack, Secretary of the R&A, had drily commented, when Norman's views on possible law suits were relayed to him, "We don't compel the players to have to go at the ball out of heavy rough any more than out of a bush." Still, the suspicion lingered that Bonallack might have been moved to steal a surreptitious look at the R&A's insurance cover.

With regard to the rough, Bonallack never ceased to insist that it was more a circumstance of the weather than the outcome of deliberate, sadistic planning. In support of that contention, Bob Jamieson, professional at Turnberry for the past quarter of a century, explained that in January, February and March, they had had rainfall of fifty-four inches – which was the highest since 1947. Spring had been late and when the weather suddenly turned hot, the growth had been dramatic. In contrast, the sparse, wispy rough of the 1977 Open, which rendered the width of the fairways largely irrelevant, had originated in the comparative droughts of 1975 and 1976.

Jack Nicklaus maintained that the rough at Muirfield in 1966 had been worse, that being the year when Doug Sanders at first refused to leave the clubhouse on the grounds that "there could be Apaches out there" and subsequently announced magnanimously that if they would just give him "the hay and lost ball concession," they could keep the prize money. But at Muirfield in 1966, said Nicklaus, you could weigh the percentages and choose your shot, which he did not consider to be the case at Turnberry in 1986.

As Nicklaus had predicted, by the last afternoon there were many places where the rough was much less punitive because it had been flattened by the passage of the galleries but, in long years of watching, I have never seen the club twist so often in the hands of seasoned professionals, the ball coming out at weirdly contorted angles even from the like of golfers of the calibre of Raymond Floyd and Seve Ballesteros.

Not even a final round of 64 softened the view of Ballesteros. "It is a good course," he reiterated, "but it was set up too severely. I hate to see the R&A following the USGA in the way they prepare a course for an Open. Over there, the fairways are softer and easier to hold, the weather mostly more predictable and consistent. The golf this past week has not been what the people came to see."

The spectacle of which Ballesteros complained had included a first day on which not one of the one hundred and fifty-three players broke the par of 70 and on which the cumulative score added up to no fewer than 1,251 over par. By the end of the second round, it had all been too much for the five amateurs, none of whom escaped the guillotine. Thus the silver medal which goes to the leading amateur after seventy-two holes found no recipient.

The 1977 champion, Tom Watson, who from the first had pointed out that the way the fairways curved compounded what he saw as the folly of making them so narrow, promised to put his views on paper in a letter to the R&A. He was as good as his word, Bonallack brandishing that letter on the morning after the championship at the R&A press conference.

In his four-page epistle, Watson was critical of the change in speed on the greens from the practice days. But again, Bonallack pointed to the part played by nature. The recent heat wave, followed by rain at the weekend, followed by the cold of much of the championship, had meant that even a greenkeeper with the skill and savvy of Turnberry's George Brown could not wholly control their pace, no matter when he cut or didn't cut, how he raised or lowered the blades.

At that same conference, Alistair Low, Chairman of the Championship Committee, conceded that the fairways had possibly been too narrow, some of them at least. There were other areas, too, where they would know better next time; notably the controversial and elusive ninth fairway, which he thought would have to be built up on the right for, as Low and Bonallack agreed, from the present wonderfully picturesque tee, the hole no longer plays as the architect, Mackenzie Ross, originally conceived.

The Ailsa course in its 1986 championship guise was far removed what most would have seen as Greg Norman's natural habitat, and the way he coped illustrated the greater patience which now more often tempers his natural aggression and confidence. "When I first saw Turnberry," he was to recall, "the deep rough, and those narrow, angled fairways, I thought, 'Oh my God.' But then I told myself to accept the fact that this was going to be a bogey week, that everyone was going to have them and that what would matter was not allowing a bogey to multiply into a double or triple."

Way back, when Norman won the Martini at Rosemount in 1977 in what was only his second tournament in Britain, he took the club back a little on the outside and then dropped it on the inside, but now his swing is very much more on the line from start to finish. His short game, and in particular his ability to manufacture shots, is greatly improved, the use he makes of his knees seemingly giving him a much softer feel. At Turnberry his putting also generally went well, the stance open as he likes to have it, the ball addressed off the toe of his

blade putter in a manner reminiscent in that respect of Bobby Locke.

On the last afternoon, one never really doubted that Norman was going to win from the moment he holed his bunker shot at the third. Some have wanted to make much of the fact that those in closest pursuit at Turnberry proved incapable of sustaining any real challenge on the last round, and so Norman was never under any great pressure. That, though, was hardly his fault, and if the great names were not hard on his heels, the fact remains that they were mostly in the field and he had already left them far in his wake.

Norman's win at Turnberry in succession to Sandy Lyle at Royal St. George's the previous year and Seve Ballesteros at St. Andrews in 1984 meant that no American had won the title since Tom Watson at Royal Birkdale in 1983. That minor statistic paled by comparison with the fact that whereas in 1977 at Turnberry eleven of the players who finished in the top twelve were Americans, this time there were only two, namely, Gary Koch, who was sixth equal, and Fuzzy Zoeller who was joint eighth.

Gary Player had advised the R&A to take no notice of the cry-babies, and both Mark McCormack and Jack Nicklaus had referred to American players as pampered. Norman, for his part, told how he had urged the stream of players emerging on the U.S. tour from college golf scholarships to play Europe, Asia and elsewhere in the world, so that they might learn to play all the shots in a variety of conditions rather than simply target golf on immaculately conditioned courses.

It would be premature to read too much into the eclipse of the Americans at Turnberry and certainly Muirfield in 1987 is likely to be much more to their taste. Nevertheless, it was interesting if nothing more that it proved the prelude to the victory on American soil of Great Britain and Ireland in the Curtis Cup which meant that of the four main Trans-Atlantic trophies, the Walker Cup, the Ryder Cup, the Curtis Cup and the PGA Cup, the Walker Cup alone now is in American hands.

In spite of the improvement of golf worldwide, a strong American presence in the Open Championship is still deemed essential, which is why the R&A have to be careful that they never so Americanise their courses as to invalidate the old saw that no champion is complete until he has proved that he can win on either side of the Atlantic.

FINAL RESULTS

Hole	1	2	3	4	5	6	7	8	9	10	11	12	13	14	15	16	17	18	Total	
Par	4	4	4	3	4	3	5	4	4	4	3	4	4	4	3	4	5	4		
GREG NORMAN																				
Round 1	4	3	4	2	6	3	5	4	4	4	4	6	4	5	3	5	4	4	74	
Round 2	4	3	3	2	5	3	3	5	4	3	2	4	4	3	3	3	4	5	63	
Round 3	3	4	4	3	3	5	4	3	5	5	3	5	4	5	3	5	5	5	74	
Round 4	4	4	3	3	5	3	5	3	4	4	4	4	4	3	3	4	5	4	69	280
GORDON J. BRAND																				
Round 1	4	4	4	3	4	3	5	5	3	4	3	5	4	6	3	4	4	3	71	
Round 2	4	3	4	3	4	2	5	5	4	3	3	4	5	4	3	4	4	4	68	
Round 3	4	4	4	3	5	4	4	4	5	5	4	4	4	4	3	4	5	5	75	
Round 4	4	4	5	3	6	2	6	5	4	4	3	3	4	4	3	4	3	4	71	285
BERNHARD LANGER																				
Round 1	3	5	4	2	5	5	5	4	4	4	3	4	5	5	4	3	3	4	72	
Round 2	5	4	5	3	4	3	5	4	4	3	3	4	3	4	3	4	5	4	70	
Round 3	5	4	4	3	4	4	5	5	4	4	3	4	5	4	3	6	5	4	76	
Round 4	4	4	5	3	4	3	4	5	4	3	3	3	3	5	3	4	4	4	68	286
IAN WOOSNAM																				
Round 1	4	5	5	3	4	4	4	6	4	3	3	4	4	3	3	4	3	4	70	
Round 2	4	4	4	3	4	4	5	6	4	4	3	4	5	4	4	4	4	4	74	
Round 3	4	4	4	3	5	2	4	4	4	3	3	4	6	5	2	4	5	4	70	
Round 4	4	5	5	3	3	3	4	5	4	5	4	5	4	3	3	4	4	4	72	286
NICK FALDO																				
Round 1	4	5	3	3	5	4	5	4	5	4	2	5	4	5	3	3	4	3	71	
Round 2	4	4	4	3	4	3	6	4	4	4	2	5	4	4	3	5	3	4	70	
Round 3	5	4	5	3	4	3	5	5	4	4	3	4	4	5	4	5	5	4	76	
Round 4	4	4	4	3	5	3	5	4	4	4	2	4	4	4	3	4	5	4	70	287
SEVE BALLESTEROS																				
Round 1	4	4	5	3	4	4	4	6	4	4	4	4	5	6	3	4	3	5	76	
Round 2	3	4	5	5	5	3	6	5	4	5	3	4	4	4	3	4	4	4	75	
Round 3	4	4	5	3	4	3	5	4	4	4	2	5	4	5	3	5	5	4	73	
Round 4	4	3	4	2	4	3	4	4	5	3	3	4	3	3	3	4	4	4	64	288
GARY KOCH																				
Round 1	4	5	5	3	5	4	5	4	4	3	2	5	4	5	4	3	4	4	73	
Round 2	3	4	3	3	5	4	5	4	5	5	3	4	4	4	4	4	4	4	72	
Round 3	5	4	5	3	4	3	4	4	4	4	2	4	5	5	3	5	5	3	72	
Round 4	4	4	4	3	4	4	4	4	4	4	3	5	4	4	3	4	5	4	71	288
FUZZY ZOELLER																				
Round 1	4	5	4	3	4	4	6	5	6	4	3	4	4	5	3	3	4	4	75	
Round 2	4	4	4	2	4	4	5	6	4	4	3	4	5	5	3	4	4	4	73	
Round 3	4	4	4	3	5	3	4	4	4	4	3	5	4	4	3	5	5	4	72	
Round 4	4	4	4	2	4	4	4	5	4	4	3	4	4	4	3	5	4	3	69	289
BRIAN MARCHBANK																				
Round 1	4	4	4	3	4	4	6	4	6	4	3	5	5	5	4	5	4	4	78	
Round 2	4	5	4	2	5	4	4	4	4	4	3	4	3	5	3	5	3	4	70	
Round 3	4	4	4	3	3	3	4	5	4	4	3	4	5	5	3	5	5	4	72	
Round 4	4	3	4	2	5	3	4	4	3	5	3	4	4	5	2	5	5	4	69	289
TSUNEYUKI NAKAJIMA																				
Round 1	4	5	4	3	6	4	4	5	4	4	3	4	4	6	3	3	4	4	74	
Round 2	4	4	5	2	5	4	5	4	4	4	2	3	4	4	2	3	4	4	67	
Round 3	4	4	4	3	4	3	4	5	3	4	3	4	5	5	3	6	4	4	71	
Round 4	6	4	5	3	4	3	4	5	4	4	3	5	4	4	3	5	6	5	77	289

RECORDS OF
THE OPEN CHAMPIONSHIP

Most victories
6, Harry Vardon, 1896-98-99-1903-11-14
5, James Braid, 1901-05-06-08-10; J.H. Taylor,
1894-95-1900-09-13; Peter Thomson, 1954-
55-56-58-65; Tom Watson, 1975-77-80-82-83

Most times runner-up or joint runner-up
7, Jack Nicklaus, 1964-67-68-72-76-77-79
6, J.H. Taylor, 1896-1904-05-06-07-14

Oldest winner
Old Tom Morris, 46 years 99 days, 1867
Roberto de Vicenzo, 44 years 93 days, 1967

Youngest winner
Young Tom Morris, 17 years 5 months 8 days, 1868
Willie Auchterlonie, 21 years 24 days, 1893
Severiano Ballesteros, 22 years 3 months 12 days, 1979

Youngest and oldest competitor
John Ball, 14 years, 1878
Gene Sarazen, 71 years 4 months 13 days, 1973

Biggest margin of victory
13 strokes, Old Tom Morris, 1862
12 strokes, Young Tom Morris, 1870
8 strokes, J.H. Taylor, 1900 and 1913; James
Braid, 1908
6 strokes, Bobby Jones, 1927; Walter Hagen, 1929;
Arnold Palmer, 1962; Johnny Miller, 1976

Lowest winning aggregates
268 (68, 70, 65, 65), Tom Watson, Turnberry, 1977
271 (68, 70, 64, 69), Tom Watson, Muirfield, 1980
275 (67, 68, 70, 70), Tom Watson, Royal Birkdale,
1983
276 (71, 69, 67, 69), Arnold Palmer, Troon, 1962
276 (68, 67, 71, 70), Tom Weiskopf, Troon, 1973
276 (72, 66, 67, 71), Bill Rogers, Sandwich, 1981
276 (69, 68, 70, 69), Severiano Ballesteros, St
Andrews, 1984

Lowest aggregates by runner-up
269 (68, 70, 65, 66), Jack Nicklaus, Turnberry, 1977
275 (68, 67, 71, 69), Lee Trevino, Muirfield, 1980

Lowest aggregate by an amateur
283 (74, 70, 71, 68), Guy Wolstenholme, St
Andrews, 1960

Lowest individual round
63, Mark Hayes, second round, Turnberry, 1977;
Isao Aoki, third round, Muirfield, 1980;
Greg Norman, second round, Turnberry, 1986

Lowest individual round by an amateur
66, Frank Stranahan, fourth round, Troon, 1950

Lowest first round
64, Craig Stadler, Royal Birkdale, 1983;
Christy O'Connor Jr, Royal St George's, 1985

Lowest second round
63, Mark Hayes, Turnberry, 1977;
Greg Norman, Turnberry, 1986

Lowest third round
63, Isao Aoki, Muirfield, 1980
64, Hubert Green and Tom Watson, Muirfield, 1980

Lowest fourth round
64, Graham Marsh, Royal Birkdale, 1983;
Severiano Ballesteros, Turnberry, 1986

Lowest first 36 holes
132 (67, 65), Henry Cotton, Sandwich, 1934
133 (67, 66), Bobby Clampett, Royal Troon, 1982

Lowest second 36 holes
130 (65, 65), Tom Watson, Turnberry, 1977

Lowest first 54 holes
202 (68, 70, 64), Tom Watson, Muirfield, 1980
203 (68, 70, 65), Jack Nicklaus and Tom Watson,
Turnberry, 1977

Lowest final 54 holes
200 (70, 65, 65), Tom Watson, Turnberry, 1977

Lowest 9 holes
28, Denis Durnian, first 9, Royal Birkdale, 1983
29, Peter Thomson and Tom Haliburton, first 9,
Royal Lytham, 1958; Tony Jacklin, first 9, St Andrews,
1970; Bill Longmuir, first 9, Royal Lytham, 1979

Winner in three decades
Gary Player, 1959, 1968, 1974

Biggest span between first and last victories
19 years, J.H. Taylor, 1894-1913
18 years, Harry Vardon, 1896-1914
15 years, Gary Player, 1959-74
14 years, Henry Cotton, 1934-48

Successive victories
4, Young Tom Morris, 1868-72. No championship
in 1871
3, Jamie Anderson, 1877-79; Bob Ferguson,
1880-82, Peter Thomson, 1954-56
2, Old Tom Morris, 1861-62; J.H. Taylor, 1894-95;
Harry Vardon, 1898-99; James Braid, 1905-06;
Bobby Jones, 1926-27; Walter Hagen, 1928-29;
Bobby Locke, 1949-50; Arnold Palmer, 1961-62;
Lee Trevino, 1971-72; Tom Watson, 1982-83

Victories by amateurs
3, Bobby Jones, 1926-27-30
2, Harold Hilton, 1892-97
1, John Ball, 1890
Roger Wethered lost a play-off in 1921

Highest number of top five finishes
16, J.H. Taylor and Jack Nicklaus
15, Harry Vardon and James Braid

Highest number of rounds under 70
28, Jack Nicklaus
16, Tom Watson, Lee Trevino
15, Peter Thomson
13, Gary Player
12, Bobby Locke, Arnold Palmer, Severiano
Ballesteros

Outright leader after every round
Willie Auchterlonie, 1893; J.H. Taylor, 1894 and
1900; James Braid, 1908; Ted Ray, 1912; Bobby
Jones, 1927; Gene Sarazen, 1932; Henry Cotton,
1934; Tom Weiskopf, 1973

Lowest round in a play-off
67, Bobby Locke, Sandwich, 1949
68, Peter Thomson, Royal Lytham, 1958; Bobby Locke, Sandwich, 1949

Record leads (since 1892)
After 18 holes:
4 strokes, James Braid, 1908; Bobby Jones, 1927; Henry Cotton, 1934; Christy O'Connor Jr, 1985
After 36 holes:
9 strokes, Henry Cotton, 1934
After 54 holes:
10 strokes, Henry Cotton, 1934
7 strokes, Tony Lema, 1964
6 strokes, James Braid, 1908
5 strokes, Arnold Palmer, 1962; Bill Rogers, 1981

Champions with each round lower than previous one
Jack White, 1904, Sandwich, 80, 75, 72, 69
James Braid, 1906, Muirfield, 77, 76, 74, 73
Ben Hogan, 1953, Carnoustie, 73, 71, 70, 68
Gary Player, 1959, Muirfield, 75, 71, 70, 68

Champion with four rounds the same
Densmore Shute, 1933, St Andrews, 73, 73, 73, 73 (excluding the play-off)

Biggest variation between rounds of a champion
14 strokes, Henry Cotton, 1934, second round 65, fourth round 79
11 strokes, Jack White, 1904, first round 80, fourth round 69; Greg Norman, 1986, first round 74, second round 63, third round 74

Biggest variation between two rounds
17 strokes, Jack Nicklaus, 1981, first round 83, second round 66; Ian Baker-Finch, 1986, first round 86, second round 69

Best comeback by champions
After 18 holes:
Harry Vardon, 1896, 11 strokes behind the leader
After 36 holes:
George Duncan, 1920, 13 strokes behind the leader
After 54 holes:
Jim Barnes, 1925, 5 strokes behind the leader

Champions with four rounds under 70
None
Arnold Palmer, 1962, Tom Watson, 1977 and 1980, and Severiano Ballesteros, 1984, had three rounds under 70

Of non-champions, Phil Rodgers, 1963, Jack Nicklaus, 1977, Lee Trevino, 1980, and Nick Faldo, 1984, had three rounds under 70

Best finishing round by a champion
65, Tom Watson, Turnberry, 1977
66, Johnny Miller, Royal Birkdale, 1976

Worst finishing round by a champion since 1920
79, Henry Cotton, Sandwich, 1934
78, Reg Whitcombe, Sandwich, 1938
77, Walter Hagen, Hoylake, 1924

Worst opening round by a champion since 1919
80, George Duncan, Deal, 1920 (he also had a second round of 80)
77, Walter Hagen, Hoylake, 1924

Best opening round by a champion
66, Peter Thomson, Royal Lytham, 1958
67, Henry Cotton, Sandwich, 1934; Tom Watson, Royal Birkdale, 1983

Biggest recovery in 18 holes by a champion
George Duncan, Deal, 1920, was 13 strokes behind the leader, Abe Mitchell, after 36 holes and level after 54

Most appearances on final day (since 1892)
30, J.H. Taylor
27, Harry Vardon, James Braid
26, Peter Thomson
24, Jack Nicklaus
23, Dai Rees
22, Henry Cotton

Championship with highest number of rounds under 70
68, Royal Birkdale, 1983

Championship since 1946 with the fewest rounds under 70
St Andrews, 1946; Hoylake, 1947; Portrush, 1951; Hoylake, 1956; Carnoustie, 1968. All had only two rounds under 70

Longest course
Carnoustie, 1968, 7252 yd (6631 m)

Courses most often used
Prestwick, 24 (but not since 1925); St Andrews, 23; Muirfield, 12; Sandwich, 11; Hoylake, 10; Royal Lytham, 7; Musselburgh and Royal Birkdale, 6; Carnoustie, 5; Royal Troon, 5; Deal and Turnberry, 2; Royal Portrush and Prince's, 1

Prize Money

Year	Total	First Prize
1860	nil	nil
1863	10	nil
1985	530,000	65,000
1986	600,000	70,000
1864	16	6
1876	20	20
1889	22	8
1891	28.50	10
1892	110	(Amateur winner)
1893	100	30
1910	125	50
1920	225	75
1927	275	100
1930	400	100
1931	500	100
1946	1,000	150
1949	1,700	300
1953	2,450	500
1954	3,500	750
1955	3,750	1,000
1958	4,850	1,000
1959	5,000	1,000
1960	7,000	1,250
1961	8,500	1,400
1963	8,500	1,500
1965	10,000	1,750
1966	15,000	2,100
1968	20,000	3,000
1969	30,000	4,250
1970	40,000	5,250
1971	45,000	5,500
1972	50,000	5,500
1975	75,000	7,500
1977	100,000	10,000
1978	125,000	12,500
1979	155,000	15,500
1980	200,000	25,000
1981	200,000	25,000
1982	250,000	32,000
1983	300,000	40,000
1984	451,000	55,000

Attendance

Year	Attendance
1962	37,098
1963	24,585
1964	35,954
1965	32,927
1966	40,182
1967	29,880
1968	51,819
1969	46,001
1970	81,593
1971	70,076
1972	84,746
1973	78,810
1974	92,796
1975	85,258
1976	92,021
1977	87,615
1978	125,271
1979	134,501
1980	131,610
1981	111,987
1982	133,299
1983	142,892
1984	193,126
1985	141,619
1986	*133,130

*Before adjustments

The largest single day attendance was 39,755 on the Saturday of the 1984 championship.

PAST RESULTS

★ Denotes amateurs

1860 Prestwick

Willie Park, Musselburgh	55	59	60	174
Tom Morris Sr, Prestwick	58	59	59	176
Andrew Strath, St Andrews				180
Robert Andrew, Perth				191
George Brown, Blackheath				192
Charles Hunter, Prestwick St Nicholas				195

1861 Prestwick

Tom Morris Sr, Prestwick	54	56	53	163
Willie Park, Musselburgh	54	54	59	167
William Dow, Musselburgh	59	58	54	171
David Park, Musselburgh	58	57	57	172
Robert Andrew, Perth	58	61	56	175
Peter McEwan, Bruntsfield	56	60	62	178

1862 Prestwick

Tom Morris Sr, Prestwick	52	55	56	163
Willie Park, Musselburgh	59	59	58	176
Charles Hunter, Prestwick	60	60	58	178
William Dow, Musselburgh	60	58	63	181
★ James Knight, Prestwick	62	61	63	186
★ J.F. Johnston, Prestwick	64	69	75	208

1863 Prestwick

Willie Park, Musselburgh	56	54	58	168
Tom Morris Sr, Prestwick	56	58	56	170
David Park, Musselburgh	55	63	54	172
Andrew Strath, St Andrews	61	55	58	174
George Brown, St Andrews	58	61	57	176
Robert Andrew, Perth	62	57	59	178

1864 Prestwick

Tom Morris Sr, Prestwick	54	58	55	167
Andrew Strath, St Andrews	56	57	56	169
Robert Andrew, Perth	57	58	60	175
Willie Park, Musselburgh	55	67	55	177
William Dow, Musselburgh	56	58	67	181
William Strath, St Andrews	60	62	60	182

1865 Prestwick

Andrew Strath, St Andrews	55	54	53	162
Willie Park, Musselburgh	56	52	56	164
William Dow, Musselburgh				171
Robert Kirk, St Andrews	64	54	55	173
Tom Morris Sr, St Andrews	57	61	56	174
★ William Doleman, Glasgow	62	57	59	178

1866 Prestwick

Willie Park, Musselburgh	54	56	59	169
David Park, Musselburgh	58	57	56	171
Robert Andrew, Perth	58	59	59	176
Tom Morris Sr, St Andrews	61	58	59	178
Robert Kirk, St Andrews	60	62	58	180
Andrew Strath, Prestwick	61	61	60	182
★ William Doleman, Glasgow	60	60	62	182

1867 Prestwick

Tom Morris Sr, St Andrews	58	54	58	170
Willie Park, Musselburgh	58	56	58	172
Andrew Strath, St Andrews	61	57	56	174
Tom Morris Jr, St Andrews	58	59	58	175
Robert Kirk, St Andrews	57	60	60	177
★ William Doleman, Glasgow	55	66	57	178

1868 Prestwick

Tom Morris Jr, St Andrews	50	55	52	157
Robert Andrew, Perth	53	54	52	159
Willie Park, Musselburgh	58	50	54	162
Robert Kirk, St Andrews	56	59	56	171
John Allan, Westward Ho!	54	55	63	172
Tom Morris Sr, St Andrews	56	62	58	176

1869 Prestwick

Tom Morris Jr, St Andrews	51	54	49	154
Tom Morris Sr, St Andrews	54	50	53	157
★ S. Mure Fergusson, Royal and Ancient	57	54	54	165
Robert Kirk, St Andrews	53	58	57	168
David Strath, St Andrews	53	56	60	169
Jamie Anderson, St Andrews	60	56	57	173

1870 Prestwick

Tom Morris Jr, St Andrews	47	51	51	149
Bob Kirk, Royal Blackheath	52	52	57	161
David Strath, St Andrews	54	49	58	161
Tom Morris Sr, St Andrews	56	52	54	162
★ William Doleman, Musselburgh	57	56	58	171
Willie Park, Musselburgh	60	55	58	173

1871 No Competition

1872 Prestwick

Tom Morris Jr, St Andrews	57	56	53	166
David Strath, St Andrews	56	52	61	169
★ William Doleman, Musselburgh	63	60	54	177
Tom Morris Sr, St Andrews	62	60	57	179
David Park, Musselburgh	61	57	61	179
Charlie Hunter, Prestwick	60	60	69	189

1873 St Andrews

Tom Kidd, St Andrews	91	88	179
Jamie Anderson, St Andrews	91	89	180
Tom Morris Jr, St Andrews	94	89	183
Bob Kirk, Royal Blackheath	91	92	183
David Strath, St Andrews	97	90	187
Walter Gourlay, St Andrews	92	96	188

1874 Musselburgh

Mungo Park, Musselburgh	75	84	159
Tom Morris Jr, St Andrews	83	78	161
George Paxton, Musselburgh	80	82	162
Bob Martin, St Andrews	85	79	164
Jamie Anderson, St Andrews	82	83	165
David Park, Musselburgh	83	83	166
W. Thomson, Edinburgh	84	82	166

1875 Prestwick

Willie Park, Musselburgh	56	59	51	166
Bob Martin, St Andrews	56	58	54	168
Mungo Park, Musselburgh	59	57	55	171
Robert Ferguson, Musselburgh	58	56	58	172
James Rennie, St Andrews	61	59	57	177
David Strath, St Andrews	59	61	58	178

1876 St Andrews

Bob Martin, St Andrews	86	90	176
David Strath, North Berwick	86	90	176
(Martin was awarded the title when Strath refused to play-off)			
Willie Park, Musselburgh	94	89	183
Tom Morris Sr, St Andrews	90	95	185
W. Thomson, Elie	90	95	185
Mungo Park, Musselburgh	95	90	185

1877 Musselburgh

Jamie Anderson, St Andrews	40	42	37	41	160
Bob Pringle, Musselburgh	44	38	40	40	162
Bob Ferguson, Musselburgh	40	40	40	44	164
William Cosgrove, Musselburgh	41	39	44	40	164
David Strath, North Berwick	45	40	38	43	166
William Brown, Musselburgh	39	41	45	41	166

1878 Prestwick

Jamie Anderson, St Andrews	53	53	51	157
Bob Kirk, St Andrews	53	55	51	159
J.O.F. Morris, St Andrews	50	56	55	161
Bob Martin, St Andrews	57	53	55	165
★ John Ball, Hoylake	53	57	55	165
Willie Park, Musselburgh	53	56	57	166
William Cosgrove, Musselburgh	55	56	55	166

1879 St Andrews

Jamie Anderson, St Andrews	84	85	169
James Allan, Westward Ho!	88	84	172
Andrew Kirkaldy, St Andrews	86	86	172
George Paxton, Musselburgh			174
Tom Kidd, St Andrews			175
Bob Ferguson, Musselburgh			176

1880 Musselburgh

Bob Ferguson, Musselburgh	81	81	162
Peter Paxton, Musselburgh	81	86	167
Ned Cosgrove, Musselburgh	82	86	168
George Paxton, Musselburgh	85	84	169
Bob Pringle, Musselburgh	90	79	169
David Brown, Musselburgh	86	83	169

1881 Prestwick

Bob Ferguson, Musselburgh	53	60	57	170
Jamie Anderson, St Andrews	57	60	56	173
Ned Cosgrove, Musselburgh	61	59	57	177
Bob Martin, St Andrews	57	62	59	178
Tom Morris Sr, St Andrews	58	65	58	181
Willie Campbell, Musselburgh	60	56	65	181
Willie Park Jr, Musselburgh	66	57	58	181

1882 St Andrews

Bob Ferguson, Musselburgh	83	88	171
Willie Fernie, Dumfries	88	86	174
Jamie Anderson, St Andrews	87	88	175
John Kirkaldy, St Andrews	86	89	175
Bob Martin, St Andrews	89	86	175
★ Fitz Boothby, St Andrews	86	89	175

1883 Musselburgh

Willie Fernie, Dumfries	75	84	159
Bob Ferguson, Musselburgh	78	80	159
(Fernie won play-off 158 to 159)			
William Brown, Musselburgh	83	77	160
Bob Pringle, Musselburgh	79	82	161
Willie Campbell, Musselburgh	80	83	163
George Paxton, Musselburgh	80	83	163

1884 Prestwick

Jack Simpson, Carnoustie	78	82	160
David Rollan, Elie	81	83	164
Willie Fernie, Felixstowe	80	84	164
Willie Campbell, Musselburgh	84	85	169
Willie Park Jr, Musselburgh	86	83	169
Ben Sayers, North Berwick	83	87	170

1885 St Andrews

Bob Martin, St Andrews	84	87	171
Archie Simpson, Carnoustie	83	89	172
David Ayton, St Andrews	89	84	173
Willie Fernie, Felixstowe	89	85	174
Willie Park Jr, Musselburgh	86	88	174
Bob Simpson, Carnoustie	85	89	174

1886 Musselburgh

David Brown, Musselburgh	79	78	157
Willie Campbell, Musselburgh	78	81	159
Ben Campbell, Musselburgh	79	81	160
Archie Simpson, Carnoustie	82	79	161
Willie Park Jr, Musselburgh	84	77	161
Thomas Gossett, Musselburgh	82	79	161
Bob Ferguson, Musselburgh	82	79	161

1887 Prestwick

Willie Park Jr, Musselburgh	82	79	161
Bob Martin, St Andrews	81	81	162
Willie Campbell, Prestwick	77	87	164
★ Johnny Laidlay, Honourable Company	86	80	166
Ben Sayers, North Berwick	83	85	168
Archie Simpson, Carnoustie	81	87	168

1888 St Andrews

Jack Burns, Warwick	86	85	171
David Anderson Jr, St Andrews	86	86	172
Ben Sayers, North Berwick	85	87	172
Willie Campbell, Prestwick	84	90	174
★ Leslie Balfour, Edinburgh	86	89	175
Andrew Kirkaldy, St Andrews	87	89	176
David Grant, North Berwick	88	88	176

1889 Musselburgh

Willie Park Jr, Musselburgh	39	39	39	38	155
Andrew Kirkaldy, St Andrews	39	38	39	39	155
(Park won play-off 158 to 163)					
Ben Sayers, North Berwick	39	40	41	39	159
★ Johnny Laidlay, Honourable Company	42	39	40	41	162
David Brown, Musselburgh	43	39	41	39	162
Willie Fernie, Troon	45	39	40	40	164

1890 Prestwick

★ John Ball, Royal Liverpool	82	82	164
Willie Fernie, Troon	85	82	167
Archie Simpson, Carnoustie	85	82	167
Willie Park Jr, Musselburgh	90	80	170
Andrew Kirkaldy, St Andrews	81	89	170
★ Horace Hutchinson, Royal North Devon	87	85	172

1891 St Andrews

Hugh Kirkaldy, St Andrews	83	83	166
Willie Fernie, Troon	84	84	168
Andrew Kirkaldy, St Andrews	84	84	168
S. Mure Fergusson, Royal and Ancient	86	84	170
W. D. More, Chester	84	87	171
Willie Park Jr, Musselburgh	88	85	173

(From 1892 the competition was extended to 72 holes)

1892 Muirfield

★ Harold Hilton, Royal Liverpool	78	81	72	74	305
★ John Ball Jr, Royal Liverpool	75	80	74	79	308
James Kirkaldy, St Andrews	77	83	73	75	308
Sandy Herd, Huddersfield	77	78	77	76	308
J. Kay, Seaton Carew	82	78	74	78	312
Ben Sayers, North Berwick	80	76	81	75	312

1893 Prestwick

Willie Auchterlonie, St Andrews	78	81	81	82	322
★ Johnny Laidlay, Honourable Company	80	83	80	81	324
Sandy Herd, Huddersfield	82	81	78	84	325
Hugh Kirkaldy, St Andrews	83	79	82	82	326
Andrew Kirkaldy, St Andrews	85	82	82	77	326
J. Kay, Seaton Carew	81	81	80	85	327
R. Simpson, Carnoustie	81	81	80	85	327

1894 Sandwich

J.H. Taylor, Winchester	84	80	81	81	326
Douglas Rolland, Limpsfield	86	79	84	82	331
Andrew Kirkaldy, St Andrews	86	79	83	84	332
A. Toogood, Eltham	84	85	82	82	333
Willie Fernie, Troon	84	84	86	80	334
Harry Vardon, Bury St Edmunds	86	86	82	80	334
Ben Sayers, North Berwick	85	81	84	84	334

1895 St Andrews

J.H. Taylor, Winchester	86	78	80	78	322
Sandy Herd, Huddersfield	82	77	82	85	326
Andrew Kirkaldy, St Andrews	81	83	84	84	332
G. Pulford, Royal Liverpool	84	81	83	87	335
Archie Simpson, Aberdeen	88	85	78	85	336
Willie Fernie, Troon	86	79	86	86	337
David Brown, Malvern	81	89	83	84	337
David Anderson, Panmure	86	83	84	84	337

1896 Muirfield

Harry Vardon, Ganton	83	78	78	77	316
J.H. Taylor, Winchester	77	78	81	80	316
(Vardon won play-off 157 to 161)					
★ Freddie G. Tait, Black Watch	83	75	84	77	319
Willie Fernie, Troon	78	79	82	80	319
Sandy Herd, Huddersfield	72	84	79	85	320
James Braid, Romford	83	81	79	80	323

1897 Hoylake

★ Harold H. Hilton, Royal Liverpool	80	75	84	75	314
James Braid, Romford	80	74	82	79	315
★ Freddie G. Tait, Black Watch	79	79	80	79	317
G. Pulford, Royal Liverpool	80	79	79	79	317
Sandy Herd, Huddersfield	78	81	79	80	318
Harry Vardon, Ganton	84	80	80	76	320

1898 Prestwick

Harry Vardon, Ganton	79	75	77	76	307
Willie Park, Musselburgh	76	75	78	79	308
★ Harold H. Hilton, Royal Liverpool	76	81	77	75	309
J.H. Taylor, Winchester	78	78	77	79	312
★ Freddie G. Tait, Black Watch	81	77	75	82	315
D. Kinnell, Leven	80	77	79	80	316

1899 Sandwich

Harry Vardon, Ganton	76	76	81	77	310
Jack White, Seaford	79	79	82	75	315
Andrew Kirkaldy, St Andrews	81	79	82	77	319
J.H. Taylor, Mid-Surrey	77	76	83	84	320
James Braid, Romford	78	78	83	84	322
Willie Fernie, Troon	79	83	82	78	322

1900 St Andrews

J.H. Taylor, Mid-Surrey	79	77	78	75	309
Harry Vardon, Ganton	79	81	80	78	317
James Braid, Romford	82	81	80	79	322
Jack White, Seaford	80	81	82	80	323
Willie Auchterlonie, St Andrews	81	85	80	80	326
Willie Park Jr, Musselburgh	80	83	81	84	328

1901 Muirfield

James Braid, Romford	79	76	74	80	309
Harry Vardon, Ganton	77	78	79	78	312
J.H. Taylor, Mid-Surrey	79	83	74	77	313
Harold H. Hilton, Royal Liverpool	89	80	75	76	320
Sandy Herd, Huddersfield	87	81	81	76	325
Jack White, Seaford	82	82	80	82	326

1902 Hoylake

Sandy Herd, Huddersfield	77	76	73	81	307
Harry Vardon, South Herts	72	77	80	79	308
James Braid, Walton Heath	78	76	80	74	308
R. Maxwell, Honourable Company	79	77	79	74	309
Tom Vardon, Ilkley	80	76	78	79	313
J.H. Taylor, Mid-Surrey	81	76	77	80	314
D. Kinnell, Leven	78	80	79	77	314
★ Harold Hilton, Royal Liverpool	79	76	81	78	314

1903 Prestwick

Harry Vardon, South Herts	73	77	72	78	300
Tom Vardon, Ilkley	76	81	75	74	306
Jack White, Sunningdale	77	78	74	79	308
Sandy Herd, Huddersfield	73	83	76	77	309
James Braid, Walton Heath	77	79	79	75	310
R. Thompson, North Berwick	83	78	77	76	314
A.H. Scott, Elie	77	77	83	77	314

1904 Sandwich

Jack White, Sunningdale	80	75	72	69	296
James Braid, Walton Heath	77	80	69	71	297
J.H. Taylor, Mid-Surrey	77	78	74	68	297
Tom Vardon, Ilkley	77	77	75	72	301
Harry Vardon, South Herts	76	73	79	74	302
James Sherlock, Stoke Poges	83	71	78	77	309

1905 St Andrews

James Braid, Walton Heath	81	78	78	81	318
J.H. Taylor, Mid-Surrey	80	85	78	80	323
R. Jones, Wimbledon	81	77	87	78	323
J. Kinnell, Purley Downs	82	79	82	81	324
Arnaud Massy, La Boulie	81	80	82	82	325
E. Gray, Littlehampton	82	81	84	78	325

1906 Muirfield

James Braid, Walton Heath	77	76	74	73	300
J.H. Taylor, Mid-Surrey	77	72	75	80	304
Harry Vardon, South Herts	77	73	77	78	305
J. Graham Jr, Royal Liverpool	71	79	78	78	306
R. Jones, Wimbledon Park	74	78	73	83	308
Arnaud Massy, La Boulie	76	80	76	78	310

1907 Hoylake

Arnaud Massy, La Boulie	76	81	78	77	312
J.H. Taylor, Mid-Surrey	79	79	76	80	314
Tom Vardon, Sandwich	81	81	80	75	317
G. Pulford, Royal Liverpool	81	78	80	78	317
Ted Ray, Ganton	83	80	79	76	318
James Braid, Walton Heath	82	85	75	76	318

1908 Prestwick

James Braid, Walton Heath	70	72	77	72	291
Tom Ball, West Lancashire	76	73	76	74	299
Ted Ray, Ganton	79	71	75	76	301
Sandy Herd, Huddersfield	74	74	79	75	302
Harry Vardon, South Herts	79	78	74	75	306
D. Kinnell, Prestwick St Nicholas	75	73	80	78	306

1909 Deal

J.H. Taylor, Mid-Surrey	74	73	74	74	295
James Braid, Walton Heath	79	73	73	74	299
Tom Ball, West Lancashire	74	75	76	76	301
C. Johns, Southdown	72	76	79	75	302
T.G. Renouf, Manchester	76	78	76	73	303
Ted Ray, Ganton	77	76	76	75	304

1910 St Andrews

James Braid, Walton Heath	76	73	74	76	299
Sandy Herd, Huddersfield	78	74	75	76	303
George Duncan, Hanger Hill	73	77	71	83	304
Laurie Ayton, Bishops Stortford	78	76	75	77	306
Ted Ray, Ganton	76	77	74	81	308
W. Smith, Mexico	77	71	80	80	308
J. Robson, West Surrey	75	80	77	76	308

1911 Sandwich

Harry Vardon, South Herts	74	74	75	80	303
Arnaud Massy, St Jean de Luz	75	78	74	76	303
(Play-off; Massy conceded at the 35th hole)					
Harold Hilton, Royal Liverpool	76	74	78	76	304
Sandy Herd, Coombe Hill	77	73	76	78	304
Ted Ray, Ganton	76	72	79	78	305
James Braid, Walton Heath	78	75	74	78	305
J.H. Taylor, Mid-Surrey	72	76	78	79	305

1912 Muirfield

Ted Ray, Oxhey	71	73	76	75	295
Harry Vardon, South Herts	75	72	81	71	299
James Braid, Walton Heath	77	71	77	78	303
George Duncan, Hanger Hill	72	77	78	78	305
Laurie Ayton, Bishops Stortford	74	80	75	79	308
Sandy Herd, Coombe Hill	76	81	76	76	309

1913 Hoylake

J.H. Taylor, Mid-Surrey	73	75	77	79	304
Ted Ray, Oxhey	73	74	81	84	312
Harry Vardon, South Herts	79	75	79	80	313
M. Moran, Dollymount	76	74	89	74	313
Johnny J. McDermott, USA	75	80	77	83	315
T. G. Renouf, Manchester	75	78	84	78	315

1914 Prestwick

Harry Vardon, South Herts	73	77	78	78	306
J.H. Taylor, Mid-Surrey	74	78	74	83	309
H.B. Simpson, St Annes Old	77	80	78	75	310
Abe Mitchell, Sonning	76	78	79	79	312
Tom Williamson, Notts	75	79	79	79	312
R.G. Wilson, Croham Hurst	76	77	80	80	313

1920 Deal

George Duncan, Hanger Hill	80	80	71	72	303
Sandy Herd, Coombe Hill	72	81	77	75	305
Ted Ray, Oxhey	72	83	78	73	306
Abe Mitchell, North Foreland	74	73	84	76	307
Len Holland, Northampton	80	78	71	79	308
Jim Barnes, USA	79	74	77	79	309

1921 St Andrews

Jock Hutchison, USA	72	75	79	70	296
★ Roger Wethered, Royal and Ancient	78	75	72	71	296
(Hutchison won play-off 150 to 159)					
T. Kerrigan, USA	74	80	72	72	298
Arthur G. Havers, West Lancs	76	74	77	72	299
George Duncan, Hanger Hill	74	75	78	74	301

1922 Sandwich

Walter Hagen, USA	76	73	79	72	300
George Duncan, Hanger Hill	76	75	81	69	301
Jim Barnes, USA	75	76	77	73	301
Jock Hutchison, USA	79	74	73	76	302
Charles Whitcombe, Dorchester	77	79	72	75	303
J.H. Taylor, Mid-Surrey	73	78	76	77	304

1923 Troon

Arthur G. Havers, Coombe Hill	73	73	73	76	295
Walter Hagen, USA	76	71	74	75	296
Macdonald Smith, USA	80	73	69	75	297
Joe Kirkwood, Australia	72	79	69	78	298
Tom Fernie, Turnberry	73	78	74	75	300
George Duncan, Hanger Hill	79	75	74	74	302
Charles A. Whitcombe, Landsdowne	70	76	74	82	302

1924 Hoylake

Walter Hagen, USA	77	73	74	77	301
Ernest Whitcombe, Came Down	77	70	77	78	302
Macdonald Smith, USA	76	74	77	77	304
F. Ball, Langley Park	78	75	74	77	304
J.H. Taylor, Mid-Surrey	75	74	79	79	307
George Duncan, Hanger Hill	74	79	74	81	308
Aubrey Boomer, St Cloud, Paris	75	78	76	79	308

1925 Prestwick

Jim Barnes, USA	70	77	79	74	300
Archie Compston, North Manchester	76	75	75	75	301
Ted Ray, Oxhey	77	76	75	73	301
Macdonald Smith, USA	76	69	76	82	303
Abe Mitchell, Unattached	77	76	75	77	305

1926 Royal Lytham

★ Robert T. Jones Jr, USA	72	72	73	74	291
Al Watrous, USA	71	75	69	78	293
Walter Hagen, USA	68	77	74	76	295
George von Elm, USA	75	72	76	72	295
Abe Mitchell, Unattached	78	78	72	71	299
T. Barber, Cavendish	77	73	78	71	299

1927 St Andrews

★ Robert T. Jones Jr, USA	68	72	73	72	285
Aubrey Boomer, St Cloud, Paris	76	70	73	72	291
Fred Robson, Cooden Beach	76	72	69	74	291
Joe Kirkwood, Australia	72	72	75	74	293
Ernest Whitcombe, Bournemouth	74	73	73	73	293
Charles Whitcombe, Crews Hill	74	76	71	75	296

1928 Sandwich

Walter Hagen, USA	75	73	72	72	292
Gene Sarazen, USA	72	76	73	73	294
Archie Compston, Unattached	75	74	73	73	295
Percy Alliss, Berlin	75	76	75	72	298
Fred Robson, Cooden Beach	79	73	73	73	298
Jose Jurado, Argentina	74	71	76	80	301
Aubrey Boomer, St Cloud, Paris	79	73	77	72	301
Jim Barnes, USA	81	73	76	71	301

1929 Muirfield

Walter Hagen, USA	75	67	75	75	292
John Farrell, USA	72	75	76	75	298
Leo Diegel, USA	71	69	82	77	299
Abe Mitchell, St Albans	72	72	78	78	300
Percy Alliss, Berlin	69	76	76	79	300
Bobby Cruickshank, USA	73	74	78	76	301

1930 Hoylake

★ Robert T. Jones Jr, USA	70	72	74	75	291
Leo Diegel, USA	74	73	71	75	293
Macdonald Smith, USA	70	77	75	71	293
Fred Robson, Cooden Beach	71	72	78	75	296
Horton Smith, USA	72	73	78	73	296
Archie Compston, Coombe Hill	74	73	68	82	297
Jim Barnes, USA	71	77	72	77	297

1931 Carnoustie

Tommy Armour, USA	73	75	77	71	296
Jose Jurado, Argentina	76	71	73	77	297
Percy Alliss, Berlin	74	78	73	73	298
Gene Sarazen, USA	74	76	75	73	298
Macdonald Smith, USA	75	77	71	76	299
John Farrell, USA	72	77	75	75	299

1932 Prince's

Gene Sarazen, USA	70	69	70	74	283
Macdonald Smith, USA	71	76	71	70	288
Arthur G. Havers, Sandy Lodge	74	71	68	76	289
Charles Whitcombe, Crews Hill	71	73	73	75	292
Percy Alliss, Beaconsfield	71	71	78	72	292
Alf Padgham, Royal Ashdown Forest	76	72	74	70	292

1933 St Andrews

Densmore Shute, USA	73	73	73	73	292
Craig Wood, USA	77	72	68	75	292
(Shute won play-off 149 to 154)					
Sid Easterbrook, Knowle	73	72	71	77	293
Gene Sarazen, USA	72	73	73	75	293
Leo Diegel, USA	75	70	71	77	293
Olin Dutra, USA	76	76	70	72	294

1934 Sandwich

Henry Cotton, Waterloo, Belgium	67	65	72	79	283
Sid Brews, South Africa	76	71	70	71	288
Alf Padgham, Sundridge Park	71	70	75	74	290
Macdonald Smith, USA	77	71	72	72	292
Joe Kirkwood, USA	74	69	71	78	292
Marcel Dallemagne, France	71	73	71	77	292

1935 Muirfield

Alf Perry, Leatherhead	69	75	67	72	283
Alf Padgham, Sundridge Park	70	72	74	71	287
Charles Whitcombe, Crews Hill	71	68	73	76	288
Bert Gadd, Brand Hall	72	75	71	71	289
Lawson Little, USA	75	71	74	69	289
Henry Picard, USA	72	73	72	75	292

1936 Hoylake

Alf Padgham, Sundridge Park	73	72	71	71	287
Jimmy Adams, Romford	71	73	71	73	288
Henry Cotton, Waterloo, Belgium	73	72	70	74	289
Marcel Dallemagne, France	73	72	75	69	289
Percy Alliss, Leeds Municipal	74	72	74	71	291
T. Green, Burnham Beeches	74	72	70	75	291
Gene Sarazen, USA	73	75	70	73	291

1937 Carnoustie

Henry Cotton, Ashridge	74	72	73	71	290
Reg Whitcombe, Parkstone	72	70	74	76	292
Charles Lacey, USA	76	75	70	72	293
Charles Whitcombe, Crews Hill	73	71	74	76	294
Bryon Nelson, USA	75	76	71	74	296
Ed Dudley, USA	70	74	78	75	297

1938 Sandwich

Reg Whitcombe, Parkstone	71	71	75	78	295
Jimmy Adams, Royal Liverpool	70	71	78	78	297
Henry Cotton, Ashridge	74	73	77	74	298
Alf Padgham, Sundridge Park	74	72	75	82	303
Jack Busson, Pannal	71	69	83	80	303
Richard Burton, Sale	71	69	78	85	303
Allan Dailey, Wanstead	73	72	80	78	303

1939 St Andrews

Richard Burton, Sale	70	72	77	71	290
Johnny Bulla, USA	77	71	71	73	292
Johnny Fallon, Huddersfield	71	73	71	79	294
Bill Shankland, Temple Newsam	72	73	72	77	294
Alf Perry, Leatherhead	71	74	73	76	294
Reg Whitcombe, Parkstone	71	75	74	74	294
Sam King, Knole Park	74	72	75	73	294

1946 St Andrews

Sam Snead, USA	71	70	74	75	290
Bobby Locke, South Africa	69	74	75	76	294
Johnny Bulla, USA	71	72	72	79	294
Charlie Ward, Little Aston	73	73	73	76	295
Henry Cotton, Royal Mid-Surrey	70	70	76	79	295
Dai Rees, Hindhead	75	67	73	80	295
Norman von Nida, Australia	70	76	74	75	295

1947 Hoylake

Fred Daly, Balmoral, Belfast	73	70	78	72	293
Reg Horne, Hendon	77	74	72	71	294
★ Frank Stranahan, USA	71	79	72	72	294
Bill Shankland, Temple Newsam	76	74	75	70	295
Richard Burton, Coombe Hill	77	71	77	71	296
Charlie Ward, Little Aston	76	73	76	72	297
Sam King, Wildernesse	75	72	77	73	297
Arthur Lees, Dore and Totley	75	74	72	76	297
Johnny Bulla, USA	80	72	74	71	297
Henry Cotton, Royal Mid-Surrey	69	78	74	76	297
Norman von Nida, Australia	74	76	71	76	297

1948 Muirfield

Henry Cotton, Royal Mid-Surrey	71	66	75	72	284
Fred Daly, Balmoral, Belfast	72	71	73	73	289
Norman von Nida, Australia	71	72	76	71	290
Roberto de Vicenzo, Argentina	70	73	72	75	290
Jack Hargreaves, Sutton Coldfield	76	68	73	73	290
Charlie Ward, Little Aston	69	72	75	74	290

1949 Sandwich

Bobby Locke, South Africa	69	76	68	70	283
Harry Bradshaw, Kilcroney, Eire	68	77	68	70	283
(Locke won play-off 135 to 147)					
Roberto de Vicenzo, Argentina	68	75	73	69	285
Sam King, Knole Park	71	69	74	72	286
Charlie Ward, Little Aston	73	71	70	72	286
Arthur Lees, Dore and Totley	74	70	72	71	287
Max Faulkner, Royal Mid-Surrey	71	71	71	74	287

1950 Troon

Bobby Locke, South Africa	69	72	70	68	279
Roberto de Vicenzo, Argentina	72	71	68	70	281
Fred Daly, Balmoral, Belfast	75	72	69	66	282
Dai Rees, South Herts	71	68	72	71	282
E. Moore, South Africa	74	68	73	68	283
Max Faulkner, Royal Mid-Surrey	73	70	70	71	283

1951 Royal Portrush

Max Faulkner, Unattached	71	70	70	74	285
Tony Cerda, Argentina	74	72	71	70	287
Charlie Ward, Little Aston	75	73	74	68	290
Fred Daly, Balmoral, Belfast	74	70	75	73	292
Jimmy Adams, Wentworth	68	77	75	72	292
Bobby Locke, South Africa	71	74	74	74	293
Bill Shankland, Temple Newsam	73	76	72	72	293
Norman Sutton, Leigh	73	70	74	76	293
Harry Weetman, Croham Hurst	73	71	75	74	293
Peter Thomson, Australia	70	75	73	75	293

1952 Royal Lytham

Bobby Locke, South Africa	69	71	74	73	287
Peter Thomson, Australia	68	73	77	70	288
Fred Daly, Balmoral, Belfast	67	69	77	76	289
Henry Cotton, Royal Mid-Surrey	75	74	74	71	294
Tony Cerda, Argentina	73	73	76	73	295
Sam King, Knole Park	71	74	74	76	295

1953 Carnoustie

Ben Hogan, USA	73	71	70	68	282
★ Frank Stranahan, USA	70	74	73	69	286
Dai Rees, South Herts	72	70	73	71	286
Peter Thomson, Australia	72	72	71	71	286
Tony Cerda, Argentina	75	71	69	71	286
Roberto de Vicenzo, Argentina	72	71	71	73	287

1954 Royal Birkdale

Peter Thomson, Australia	72	71	69	71	283
Sid Scott, Carlisle City	76	67	69	72	284
Dai Rees, South Herts	72	71	69	72	284
Bobby Locke, South Africa	74	71	69	70	284
Jimmy Adams, Royal Mid-Surrey	73	75	69	69	286
Tony Cerda, Argentina	71	71	73	71	286
J. Turnesa, USA	72	72	71	71	286

1955 St Andrews

Peter Thomson, Australia	71	68	70	72	281
Johnny Fallon, Huddersfield	73	67	73	70	283
Frank Jowle, Edgbaston	70	71	69	74	284
Bobby Locke, South Africa	74	69	70	72	285
Tony Cerda, Argentina	73	71	71	71	286
Ken Bousfield, Coombe Hill	71	75	70	70	286
Harry Weetman, Croham Hurst	71	71	70	74	286
Bernard Hunt, Hartsbourne	70	71	74	71	286
Flory van Donck, Belgium	71	72	71	72	286

1956 Hoylake

Peter Thomson, Australia	70	70	72	74	286
Flory van Donck, Belgium	71	74	70	74	289
Roberto de Vicenzo, Argentina	71	70	79	70	290
Gary Player, South Africa	71	76	73	71	291
John Panton, Glenbervie	74	76	72	70	292
Henry Cotton, Temple	72	76	71	74	293
E. Bertolino, Argentina	69	72	76	76	293

1957 St Andrews

Bobby Locke, South Africa	69	72	68	70	279
Peter Thomson, Australia	73	69	70	70	282
Eric Brown, Buchanan Castle	67	72	73	71	283
Angel Miguel, Spain	72	72	69	72	285
David Thomas, Sudbury	72	74	70	70	286
Tom Haliburton, Wentworth	72	73	68	73	286
★ Dick Smith, Prestwick	71	72	72	71	286
Flory van Donck, Belgium	72	68	74	72	286

1958 Royal Lytham

Peter Thomson, Australia	66	72	67	73	278
David Thomson, Sudbury	70	68	69	71	278
(Thomson won play-off 139 to 143)					
Eric Brown, Buchanan Castle	73	70	65	71	279
Christy O'Connor, Killarney	67	68	73	71	279
Flory van Donck, Belgium	70	70	67	74	281
Leopoldo Ruiz, Argentina	71	65	72	73	281

1959 Muirfield

Gary Player, South Africa	75	71	70	68	284
Flory van Donck, Belgium	70	70	73	73	286
Fred Bullock, Prestwick St Ninians	68	70	74	74	286
Sid Scott, Roehampton	73	70	73	71	287
Christy O'Connor, Royal Dublin	73	74	72	69	288
★ Reid Jack, Dullatur	71	75	68	74	288
Sam King, Knole Park	70	74	68	76	288
John Panton, Glenbervie	72	72	71	73	288

1960 St Andrews

Kel Nagle, Australia	69	67	71	71	278
Arnold Palmer, USA	70	71	70	68	279
Bernard Hunt, Hartsbourne	72	73	71	66	282
Harold Henning, South Africa	72	72	69	69	282
Robert de Vicenzo, Argentina	67	67	75	73	282
★ Guy Wolstenholme, Sunningdale	74	70	71	68	283

1961 Royal Birkdale

Arnold Palmer, USA	70	73	69	72	284
Dai Rees, South Herts	68	74	71	72	285
Christy O'Connor, Royal Dublin	71	77	67	73	288
Neil Coles, Coombe Hill	70	77	69	72	288
Eric Brown, Unattached	73	76	70	70	289
Kel Nagle, Australia	68	75	75	71	289

1962 Troon

Arnold Palmer, USA	71	69	67	69	276
Kel Nagle, Australia	71	71	70	70	282
Brian Huggett, Romford	75	71	74	69	289
Phil Rodgers, USA	75	70	72	72	289
Bob Charles, NZ	75	70	70	75	290
Sam Snead, USA	76	73	72	71	292
Peter Thomson, Australia	70	77	75	70	292

1963 Royal Lytham

Bob Charles, NZ	68	72	66	71	277
Phil Rodgers, USA	67	68	73	69	277
(Charles won play-off 140 to 148)					
Jack Nicklaus, USA	71	67	70	70	278
Kel Nagle, Australia	69	70	73	71	283
Peter Thomson, Australia	67	69	71	78	285
Christy O'Connor, Royal Dublin	74	68	76	68	286

1964 St Andrews

Tony Lema, USA	73	68	68	70	279
Jack Nicklaus, USA	76	74	66	68	284
Roberto de Vicenzo, Argentina	76	72	70	67	285
Bernard Hunt, Hartsbourne	73	74	70	70	287
Bruce Devlin, Australia	72	72	73	73	290
Christy O'Connor, Royal Dublin	71	73	74	73	291
Harry Weetman, Selsdon Park	72	71	75	73	291

1965 Royal Birkdale

Peter Thomson, Australia	74	68	72	71	285
Christy O'Connor, Royal Dublin	69	73	74	71	287
Briann Huggett, Romford	73	68	76	70	287
Robert de Vicenzo, Argentina	74	69	73	72	288
Kel Nagle, Australia	74	70	73	72	289
Tony Lema, USA	68	72	75	74	289
Bernard Hunt, Hartsbourne	74	74	70	71	289

1966 Muirfield

Jack Nicklaus, USA	70	67	75	70	282
David Thomas, Dunham Forest	72	73	69	69	283
Doug Sanders, USA	71	70	72	70	283
Gary Player, South Africa	72	74	71	69	286
Bruce Devlin, Australia	73	69	74	70	286
Kel Nagle, Australia	72	68	76	70	286
Phil Rodgers, USA	74	66	70	76	286

1967 Hoylake

Robert de Vicenzo, Argentina	70	71	67	70	278
Jack Nicklaus, USA	71	69	71	69	280
Clive Clark, Sunningdale	70	73	69	72	284
Gary Player, South Africa	72	71	67	74	284
Tony Jacklin, Potters Bar	73	69	73	70	285
Sebastian Miguel, Spain	72	74	68	72	286
Harold Henning, South Africa	74	70	71	71	286

1968 Carnoustie

Gary Player, South Africa	74	71	71	73	289
Jack Nicklaus, USA	76	69	73	73	291
Bob Charles, NZ	72	72	71	76	291
Billy Casper, USA	72	68	74	78	292
Maurice Bembridge, Little Aston	71	75	73	74	293
Brian Barnes, Burnham & Berrow	70	74	80	71	295
Neil Coles, Coombe Hill	75	76	71	73	295
Gay Brewer, USA	74	73	72	76	295

1969 Royal Lytham

Tony Jacklin, Potters Bar	68	70	70	72	280
Bob Charles, NZ	66	69	75	72	282
Peter Thomson, Australia	71	70	70	72	283
Roberto de Vicenzo, Argentina	72	73	66	72	283
Christy O'Connor, Royal Dublin	71	65	74	74	284
Jack Nicklaus, USA	75	70	68	72	285
Davis Love Jr, USA	70	73	71	71	285

1970 St Andrews

Jack Nicklaus, USA	68	69	73	73	283
Doug Sanders, USA	68	71	71	73	283
(Nicklaus won play-off 72 to 73)					
Harold Henning, South Africa	67	72	73	73	285
Lee Trevino, USA	68	68	72	77	285
Tony Jacklin, Potters Bar	67	70	73	76	286
Neil Coles, Coombe Hill	65	74	72	76	287
Peter Oosterhuis, Dulwich and Sydenham	73	69	69	76	287

1971 Royal Birkdale

Lee Trevino, USA	69	70	69	70	278
Lu Liang Huan, Taiwan	70	70	69	70	279
Tony Jacklin, Potters Bar	69	70	70	71	280
Craig de Foy, Coombe Hill	72	72	68	69	281
Jack Nicklaus, USA	71	71	72	69	283
Charles Coody, USA	74	71	70	68	283

1972 Muirfield

Lee Trevino, USA	71	70	66	71	278
Jack Nicklaus, USA	70	72	71	66	279
Tony Jacklin, Potters Bar	69	72	67	72	280
Doug Sanders, USA	71	71	69	70	281
Brian Barnes, Fairway D R	71	72	69	71	283
Gary Player, South Africa	71	71	76	67	285

1973 Troon

Tom Weiskopf, USA	68	67	71	70	276
Neil Coles, Holiday Inns	71	72	70	66	279
Johnny Miller, USA	70	68	69	72	279
Jack Nicklaus, USA	69	70	76	65	280
Bert Yancey, USA	69	69	73	70	281
Peter Butler, Golf Domes	71	72	74	69	286

1974 Royal Lytham

Gary Player, South Africa	69	68	75	70	282
Peter Oosterhuis, Pacific Harbour	71	71	73	71	286
Jack Nicklaus, USA	74	72	70	71	287
Hubert Green, USA	71	74	72	71	288
Danny Edwards, USA	70	73	76	73	292
Lu Liang Huan, Taiwan	72	72	75	73	292

1975 Carnoustie

Tom Watson, USA	71	67	69	72	279
Jack Newton, Australia	69	71	65	74	279
(Watson won play-off 71 to 72)					
Bobby Cole, South Africa	72	66	66	76	280
Jack Nicklaus, USA	69	71	68	72	280
Johnny Miller, USA	71	69	66	74	280
Graham Marsh, Australia	72	67	71	71	281

1976 Royal Birkdale

Johnny Miller, USA	72	68	73	66	279
Jack Nicklaus, USA	74	70	72	69	285
Severiano Ballesteros, Spain	69	69	73	74	285
Raymond Floyd, USA	76	67	73	70	286
Mark James, Burghley Park	76	72	74	66	288
Hubert Green, USA	72	70	78	68	288
Christy O'Connor Jr, Shannon	69	73	75	71	288
Tom Kite, USA	70	74	73	71	288
Tommy Horton, Royal Jersey	74	69	72	73	288

1977 Turnberry

Tom Watson, USA	68	70	65	65	268
Jack Nicklaus, USA	68	70	65	66	269
Hubert Green, USA	72	66	74	67	279
Lee Trevino, USA	68	70	72	70	280
Ben Crenshaw, USA	71	69	66	75	281
George Burns, USA	70	70	72	69	281

1978 St. Andrews

Jack Nicklaus, USA	71	72	69	69	281
Simon Owen, NZ	70	75	67	71	283
Ben Crenshaw, USA	70	69	73	71	283
Raymond Floyd, USA	69	75	71	68	283
Tom Kite, USA	72	69	72	70	283
Peter Oosterhuis, GB	72	70	69	73	284

1979 Royal Lytham

Severiano Ballesteros, Spain	73	65	75	70	283
Jack Nicklaus, USA	72	69	73	72	286
Ben Crenshaw, USA	72	71	72	71	286
Mark James, Burghley Park	76	69	69	73	287
Rodger Davis, Australia	75	70	70	73	288
Hale Irwin, USA	68	68	75	78	289

1980 Muirfield

Tom Watson, USA	68	70	64	69	271
Lee Trevino, USA	68	67	71	69	275
Ben Crenshaw, USA	70	70	68	69	277
Jack Nicklaus, USA	73	67	71	69	280
Carl Mason, Unattached	72	69	70	69	280

1981 Sandwich

Bill Rogers, USA	72	66	67	71	276
Bernhard Langer, Germany	73	67	70	70	280
Mark James, Otley	72	70	68	73	283
Raymond Floyd, USA	74	70	69	70	283
Sam Torrance, Caledonian Hotel	72	69	73	70	284
Bruce Leitzke, USA	76	69	71	69	285
Manuel Pinero, Spain	73	74	68	70	285

1982 Troon

Tom Watson, USA	69	71	74	70	284
Peter Oosterhuis, GB	74	67	74	70	285
Nick Price, South Africa	69	69	74	73	285
Nick Faldo, Glynwed Ltd	73	73	71	69	286
Des Smyth, EAL Tubes	70	69	74	73	286
Tom Purtzer, USA	76	66	75	69	286
Massy Kuramoto, Japan	71	73	71	71	286

1983 Royal Birkdale

Tom Watson, USA	67	68	70	70	275
Hale Irwin, USA	69	68	72	67	276
Andy Bean, USA	70	69	70	67	276
Graham Marsh, Australia	69	70	74	64	277
Lee Trevino, USA	69	66	73	70	278
Severiano Ballesteros, Spain	71	71	69	68	279
Harold Henning, South Africa	71	69	70	69	279

1984 St. Andrews

Severiano Ballesteros, Spain	69	68	70	69	276
Bernhard Langer, Germany	71	68	68	71	278
Tom Watson, USA	71	68	66	73	278
Fred Couples, USA	70	69	74	68	281
Lanny Wadkins, USA	70	69	73	69	281
Greg Norman, Australia	67	74	74	67	282
Nick Faldo, Glynwed Int.	69	68	76	69	282

1985 Sandwich

Sandy Lyle, Scotland	68	71	73	70	282
Payne Stewart, USA	70	75	70	68	283
Jose Rivero, Spain	74	72	70	68	284
Christy O'Connor Jr, Ireland	64	76	72	72	284
Mark O'Meara, USA	70	72	70	72	284
David Graham, Australia	68	71	70	75	284
Bernhard Langer, Germany	72	69	68	75	284

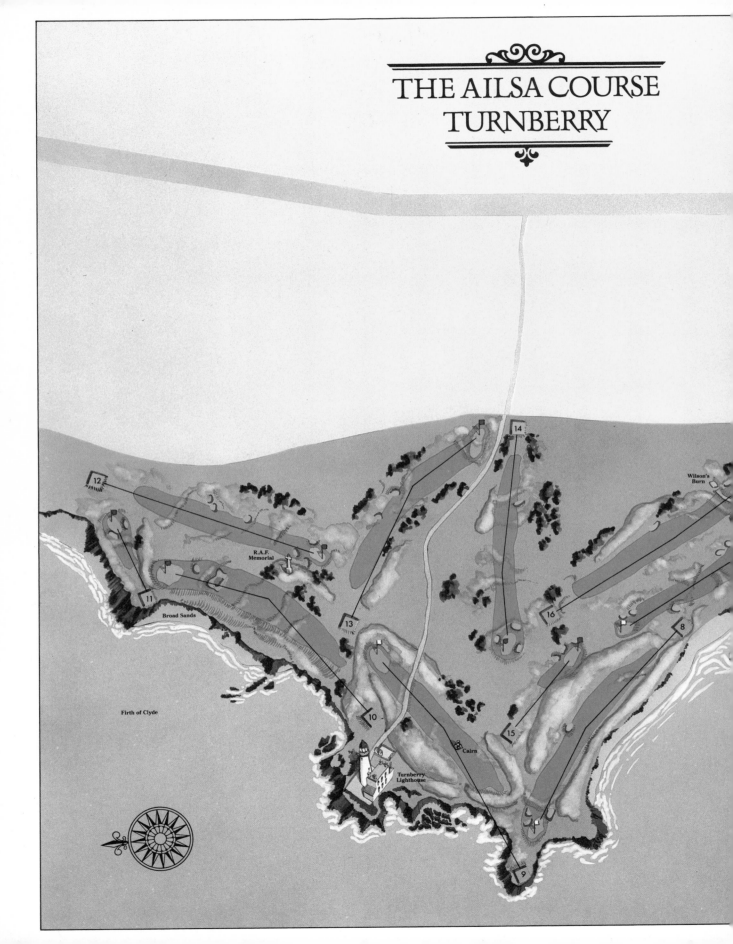

THE AILSA COURSE
TURNBERRY

Wilson's Burn

12

R.A.F.
Memorial

14

11

Broad Sands

13

8

16

Firth of Clyde

10

15

Cairn

Turnberry
Lighthouse

9